Using PCs
on Board

second edition

Other titles of interest

Understanding Weatherfax 2nd edition by Mike Harris
ISBN: 0-7136-6122-4

How do you turn the symbols on a weather chart into a meaningful forecast? Armed with this book and a current weatherfax chart you have all of the essentials for making your own forecast, no matter where you are in the world. Includes information on receiving equipment and software, interpreting synoptic chart features, personal forecasting, world weather patterns and tracking and avoiding tropical storms. New to this edition are case studies on the 1991 'Perfect Storm' and the 1998 Sydney to Hobart Race.

Using GPS 3rd edition by Conrad Dixon. Revised by Geoff Hales
ISBN: 0-7136-5835-5

Using GPS aims to help owners get the best from their sets and make full use of the facilities available, whether simply position fixing and course setting, or interfacing with integrated navigation systems. This book shows how GPS can make a trip both safer and quicker for both sailors and motorboaters with advice on how to use and interpret the data received, test it for accuracy and troubleshoot when necessary. Eleven sets are reviewed function by function.

Using Radar by Robert Avis
ISBN: 0-7136-5252-7

Using Radar is a clear and concise guide which will help potential purchasers make the right choice of equipment for their boats, as well as guiding existing owners through the wide range of facilities available. This book explains how radar works; how to install, set up and adjust equipment; radar's capabilities, inaccuracies and errors; how to interpret the information displayed; screen orientation; collision avoidance; blind pilotage; and integrating radar with other navigation aids.

GMDSS 2nd edition by Denise Brehaut
ISBN: 0-7136-6224-7

Anyone with GMDSS equipment on board their vessel will need an operator's license. This book explains the operation of the system as a whole and the procedures involved, as well as covering the syllabi of the General Operator's Certificate (GOC), the Restricted Operator's Certificate (ROC), the Long Range Certificate (LRC) and the Short Range Certificate (SRC). This is an invaluable reference for both exam candidates and equipment users alike.

Using PCs on Board

second edition

Rob Buttress & Tim Thornton

ADLARD COLES NAUTICAL
London

This edition published 2002 by Adlard Coles Nautical
an imprint of A & C Black Publishers Ltd
37 Soho Square, London W1D 3QZ
www.adlardcoles.com

First published 2000 by Adlard Coles Nautical

ISBN 0-7136-6210-7

A & C Black uses paper produced with elemental chlorine-free pulp, harvested
from managed sustainable forests

Typeset by Rob Buttress in Optimum 10/12

Printed and bound in Great Britain by The Cromwell Press, Trowbridge, Wiltshire

Note: While all reasonable care has been taken in the publication of this book,
the publisher takes no responsibility for the use of the methods or products
described in the book.

Contents

Acknowledgements

The authors are grateful for permission to use the following photographs and illustrations:

Bonito Systems – Pages 68, 70
Bernard Clack – Page 113
Euronav Ltd – Pages 23, 37, 44, 50
ICS Electronics Ltd – Pages 67, 72, 73
Informatique et Mer – Pages 23, 37
Intel Corporation – Page 99
Iomega Corporation – Page 102
IPC Magazines Ltd – Page 87
Neptune Navigation Systems – Page 50
Lightmaster Software – Page 83
Magellan – Page 28
Maptech UK Ltd – Pages 23, 32, 43, 138
Marine Computing International Ltd – Pages 22, 48, 53, 54, 71, 81, 85, 97, 112
Merlin Equipment Ltd – Page 122
Over The Horizon – Page 77
PC Maritime Ltd – Page 17, 84
David Parrott – Page 105, 106, 107, 108, 109
Raymarine – Page 75
SCS Mare – Page 41, 79, 80
Seawave LLC – Page 76
Techman – Page 78
Transas Nautic – Page 35, 40, 42, 76

In addition, the authors would like to thank James Hortop of Merlin Equipment for information on inverters and power supplies; also Nichola Woodward, Pamela Lawson, Henk van Beever and the team at Adlard Coles for painstaking proofreading.

Electronic chart images reproduced courtesy of the Controller of Her Majesty's Stationery Office United Kingdom Hydrographic Office and others. Marine software systems including electronic charting systems are not a replacement for traditional navigational methods and should be used prudently. Chart images included in this book are not for navigation.

All trademarks are acknowledged as being the property of their respective owners.

About this book

Introduction to the second edition

We wrote the first edition of 'Using PCs on Board' because in our professional and in our yachting lives, it was clear that though PC technology had an obvious place on board sailing and motor yachts, strangely, yachtsmen and women were reluctant to 'take the plunge' and actually take their valuable PC afloat.

That edition challenged the fallacy that 'computers and boats don't mix' and demonstrated the many ways PCs could help people enjoy their sailing more.

In the last couple of years, things have certainly changed, and the chances are that you already know someone who regularly uses a PC for some aspect of their yachting. Roughly half of yachtsmen using PCs will have had a happy experience, the other half less so.

This edition is intended to help keep you in the first half, to offer good, reliable advice on choosing and using PCs and marine software. It outlines what PCs can do for you and more importantly will give you an appreciation of their limitations; it may even help you avoid making expensive mistakes.

You may already have a laptop computer and want to know what it can do for you, or wish to extend its capabilities, or you may be thinking of buying a computer as an alternative to expensive, dedicated instruments.

While marine software has got much better in the last couple of years, there are now so many more brands to choose from (offering a bewildering array of features that you may or may not want or need), that making the right choice is probably harder than it was. Hopefully this book will make your choice easier, reassure you that you have made the right decision, or at least show you where you have gone wrong so that you can get it right next time!

This book is **not** written for computer buffs or enthusiasts. It is written for ordinary cruising and racing sailors and powerboaters, using everyday terms. It includes a glossary explaining key terms and topics. Even if you are generally familiar with computers, you should still find this book useful because it is not an everyday computer manual, but instead attempts to explain the technology in a way that is relevant to boat users.

In the fast moving computer world, there is nothing so constant as change — processors get faster, storage gets more affordable seemingly every day, so be sure to use this book in conjunction with an up-to-date computer magazine if choosing a system for yourself. Alternatively, work with a marine computing company if you believe you have a specialist requirement.

Regarding capacities and speeds quoted in this book, as we go to press in 2002, 'the future' means the next three or four years.

Finally, PC doesn't just stand for 'personal computer'! In the interests of being 'politically correct' and not offending anyone, we have tried to use terms that are not gender-specific. We could not quite bring ourselves to use that bland PC term 'boater', so where we refer to 'yachtsman/men' etc, we mean all sailors, whatever their sex. Similarly, the term 'yachtsman' refers to those of you who take pleasure from using any reasonably sized boat on the water, whether propelled primarily by sails, or by a motor.

About the Authors

Rob Buttress has sailed for over twenty years. After completing his studies he joined the computer industry to learn the ropes from the ground up, working on programming, hardware and sales and marketing projects.

After a career break spent blue-water cruising, Rob held senior marketing posts with leading marine navigational software companies during the early days of marine software development. Rob is now a professional yachtmaster, skippering yachts in the luxury charter sector – and using marine software on a daily basis. He is also a member of the Royal Institute of Navigation and the Professional Yachtsmen's Association.

Tim Thornton studied naval architecture, and worked on yacht design and race handicapping systems. After taking a degree in maths and computing, he became a marine computing research scientist for IBM as well as one of the pioneers in on board computer systems for racing yachts.

Tim now runs a company specialising in marine computing systems. His experience ranges from supplying systems to offshore racers in events such as the *Around Alone* and *Volvo Round the World Races* through to superyachts, as well as providing for the needs of the normal weekend sailor or club racer.

Tim is also the author of '*The Offshore Yacht*' and '*The Small Offshore Yacht*'.

Do you want to have a PC on board anyway?

Throughout the late 1980s and early 1990s, there *were* yachtsmen who were brave, rich or enthusiastic enough to take computers on board their yachts or motorboats. Computers were very expensive, the programs were relatively amateurish and fairly unreliable, and electrical power was in short supply. You wonder why they ever bothered in the first place!

The reason is that yachtsmen quickly found such systems really aided their sailing, giving accurate, timely information and taking a lot of the slog out of navigational calculations. Cruisers could spend more time actually enjoying the sailing; racers became much more competitive because they could identify trends in real time and analyse their boat and crew's performance better than ever before.

Coupled with this, two key factors occurred in the early nineties. Firstly, affordable GPS (Global Positioning System) navigators became commonplace – many of these were able to transmit position, course and speed information to other devices, including PCs. Secondly, the massive explosion in PC sales caused by such things as the Internet and multimedia really brought prices down.

Not only have PCs have become genuinely affordable – they have also become much more reliable and powerful; and the software running on them has become far, far better than was the case even a very few years ago.

Often with computers, people would rather 'wait and see' before committing to a purchase, in the hope that something better comes along soon at a lower price. The message of this book is **don't** – good, affordable and reliable systems are here **now**. Also, where some older programs were designed to lock you into particular (often proprietary) technologies, nowadays they are often designed to be 'open', allowing you choice and flexibility, and a lower-cost upgrade path for the future.

There's never been a better time to get started. So, if you could do with an extra crew member to help you with tides, route planning, plotting and logging, performance analysis, weather information, communications, even astro sight reductions, read on.

Size *is* important...

There are obviously some vessels that are simply too small or 'too wet' to have a computer on board. There is typically a minimum size of boat that might use a PC on board – a couple of years ago, that might have been 15 metres LOA (45 feet), but nowadays it's common to see boats as small as 8½ metres LOA (25 feet), some even less, with PCs on board.

Even if you have a small half-decked fishing boat, you may still be able to use the power of a PC – to work out the tides, for example, or to plan fishing trips – but this would be done at home, not on the boat. You can 'download' waypoints from electronic charting systems into a hand-held GPS, or print out the tides for the day onto paper, seal it into a polythene pocket and take that with you.

So how small is too small? This is a difficult question to answer, and will be a commonsense decision that you make for yourself, based on the size and general characteristics of your boat as well as the depth of your pocket. To help you decide, speak to other sailors – marinas and yacht club bars are great places to pick other people's brains, and the chances are that a fellow club member has useful advice to pass on.

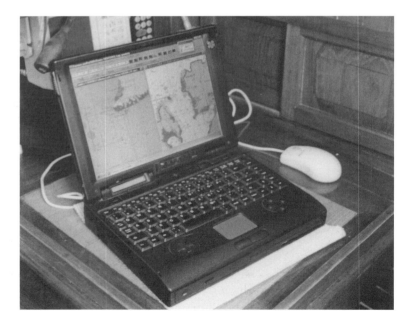

A simple set-up: a laptop PC connected to a GPS set and running chart plotting software

What do you need?

The most basic set-up, and certainly the most common, is a laptop PC, powered directly by the boat's battery supply or through a small inverter, probably connected to a hand-held GPS navigator, and with basic software loaded. Even this simple set-up is extremely powerful. This could be used for simple chart plotting and calculation-based tasks such as working out the state of the tide at a given time or reducing sextant observations for position lines. Word processing software lets you keep a narrative log, or you could use yacht management software to detail locations of stores, spares etc; with other familiar 'office-type' software, for example a spreadsheet, you could keep the boat's accounts; in harbour, multimedia CD-ROMs, DVDs and computer games can keep the children (and adults) amused.

This kind of set-up can be bought very inexpensively, certainly for less than the cost of a colour 'chart plotter' or a couple of navigation instrument repeater heads. It doesn't stop there though: the wonderful thing about using a PC is that it's remarkably cheap to add features; for a little extra, you can have a fully featured and very sophisticated system, without having to trade in your PC each time you want to add a function.

What else can you do with it?

On top of the basic system described above, it's simple to connect a PC to the following equipment:

- **Other electronic navigation instruments** (log, depth sounder, wind, compass, barometer, temperature, etc) – This can allow you to display *and keep a log* of information provided by your instruments – a great convenience and really useful for performance analysis.

- **Radar** – Several chart plotting systems can export waypoints to a suitable radar, or even a 'marker flag' (representing a known point on the chart) which appears on the radar screen as a 'lollipop'. Many can even be interfaced with ARPA or Mini ARPA radar sets to show moving vessel targets on top of the electronic chart. Older systems could obscure important chart information, but with improved display techniques (that skilfully blend the radar and chart image) and larger, higher resolution screens this is no longer a problem.

- **Autopilot** – Using chart plotting software you can quickly plan and re-plan routes, and some systems even take the tide, ocean currents and forecast weather into account – imagine being able to feed a realistic course to steer to your autopilot after every waypoint change.

- **Single Side Band (SSB) receiver** – Connect your PC to the audio output of your SSB to receive weatherfax (detailed weather maps); receive radio-telex and NAVTEX using the same connection, all free of charge. With an SSB transceiver and a suitable modem, you can even send worldwide radio-telex and e-mail messages at very low cost.

- **Mobile phone** – Send and receive faxes or download information from the Internet using a 'data enabled' cellphone. In most of the world, the GSM cellular 'phone network provides seamless coverage within range of (land-based) transmitters. In the US and Caribbean, comparable systems exist and can even be rented if you are not cruising in an area for long.

- **Satcom** – Out of cellphone range? Connect to a satellite communication unit for global e-mail, send and receive faxes or even surf the World Wide Web.

- **Digital cameras** – With digital still and video cameras now commonplace and affordable, it's easy to store the pictures on your PC and view your holiday snaps on-screen. E-mailing a photograph of damage to your insurer may even prompt faster payment if you need to make a claim!

- **Television** – In addition to being able to play DVD movies, many PCs can have TV tuner cards fitted, so they can receive terrestrial TV broadcasts in PAL, NTSC or SECAM formats. Or connect to a satellite TV decoder and dish (the dish can be gyro-stabilised for use at sea, or when in harbour, simply mount a dish on the dock).

- **Surveillance cameras** – Increasingly, larger yachts are fitting weatherproof cameras that may be remotely controlled from the PC. These can be used for security, or to monitor machinery spaces, even underwater, trained on the propellor. New infra-red stabilised systems even claim they may help prevent collisions with whales or containers.

- **Printer** – Though not essential, a printer on board really helps, whether it is to produce hard-copy of weatherfaxes, a copy of the log, or pilotage information to use (in a polypocket) in the cockpit when approaching an unfamiliar landfall.

1 ▪ The PC: Hardware, Software and Data

What is a PC?

Many people use PC as a general term when referring to many different kinds of personal computers. However, a widely accepted definition (which we adopted for the purposes of this book) is:

'A PC is a computer, running one of Microsoft's desktop operating systems (Windows 98/Me/XP/NT or 2000), equipped with a USB port and possibly an RS232 serial port and a parallel printer port.'

Though a bit of a mouthful, this definition is important because there are other types of personal computer that, for the sake of brevity, are not covered in detail in this book. Though different types of personal computer may have a place on your vessel, the above definition will, in the authors' opinion, give you the greatest possible choice in terms of the uses to which you may put the system. It should also allow you to easily and cost-effectively keep your system up-to-date. See *Appendix 1 – Other Types of Personal Computer,* for a brief description of alternative computers that you may consider using on board.

What's in the box?

What's in the box?

There are three basic elements to any PC system that you might use on board. Described in more detail later on, briefly they are:

Hardware – The physical components that make up the PC: screen, keyboard, mouse, disk drives etc. See chapter 9, Choosing a PC System, for an in-depth discussion of the various parts of a PC and advice on how to interpret manufacturers' specifications.

System software – Usually, your PC also has an 'operating system' installed when you buy it; all PCs need an operating system to provide you with an easy and consistent way of controlling them.

Application software – So called to distinguish it from the operating system, this is usually called just 'software' or a 'program'.

Being able to run application software is why you bought your PC in the first place, and provides you with the tools to do a particular job. For example, you might buy a program to work out tide times, a full electronic-charting system, or software to write letters (a word processor). You can buy as many different programs for your PC as you like so long as they will work with your operating system and so long as the PC is powerful enough to run them. Unless you purchase your PC from a marine computing specialist, it is unlikely that it will be supplied with marine application software.

Chapters 2 to 8 explain various types of application software that you might use on board, and chapter 9 advises you on choosing a PC that is suitable for the program(s) you want to use.

Data –Whatever software you have purchased, it will need data to work with. Data is really a computer word for 'information', and is something you supply yourself (eg typing a letter in a word processor) or purchase (eg electronic charts or tidal information).

Some application software will include at least some of the data it needs; for example, it may have tide-table information included.

Tip – Useful data usually belongs to someone and may be copyrighted because it is very expensive to provide. Thus watch out for software that uses time-limited data or that has data in it for a particular geographical area – the chances are that you will need to buy updates or enhanced coverage. This is not usually unreasonable, but always ask if the software will allow you to add data yourself should you not wish to buy updates.

What else is required?

It is usual that when you purchase a PC, it is supplied with all the hardware required. It will probably also have an operating system (usually a version of Microsoft's Windows) installed. Often, home PC suppliers also include what they term 'bundles' of application software, already installed on the PC's hard disk. Most 'bundled' software is of limited use on board and, if not pre-installed, should be left in the box, unless you believe you have a use for it.

To have a useful system on board, you will need to purchase application software and data. You may also need to buy an 'inverter', to power it from your boat's 12V or 24V batteries; and an 'interface' cable, to connect the PC to on board instrument(s) such as a GPS set. These issues are described in more detail in chapter 10, Installing your PC.

The tools: software and data

One of the great things about PCs is that they can be used for virtually anything that involves the processing of words or numbers. That said, there are occasions when 'doing it by computer' is just not worth the effort – sometimes good old pen and paper, or even the humble human brain, is the best solution. These areas include things associated with human judgement and experience, or where source data isn't currently available or accurate enough.

With suitable software, PCs can be useful for many different tasks on board, especially if connected to external equipment

Nevertheless, whilst PCs can't grind winches, they are particularly adept at handling repetitive calculations accurately and at processing raw data and presenting it as 'real information' so that the user can make decisions based on it.

There are many areas of leisure boating where the power of PCs will help you enjoy your sport more, or even become better at it.

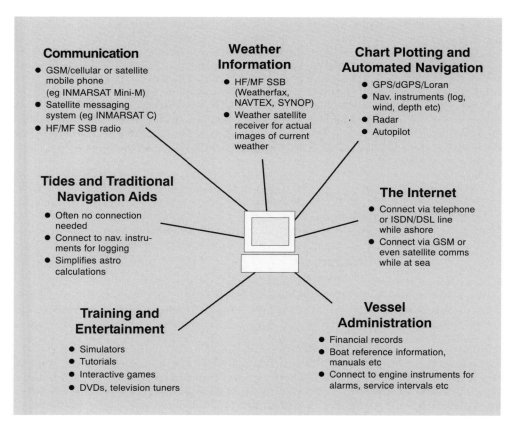

Communication
- GSM/cellular or satellite mobile phone (eg INMARSAT Mini-M)
- Satellite messaging system (eg INMARSAT C)
- HF/MF SSB radio

Weather Information
- HF/MF SSB (Weatherfax, NAVTEX, SYNOP)
- Weather satellite receiver for actual images of current weather

Chart Plotting and Automated Navigation
- GPS/dGPS/Loran
- Nav. instruments (log, wind, depth etc)
- Radar
- Autopilot

Tides and Traditional Navigation Aids
- Often no connection needed
- Connect to nav. instruments for logging
- Simplifies astro calculations

The Internet
- Connect via telephone or ISDN/DSL line while ashore
- Connect via GSM or even satellite comms while at sea

Training and Entertainment
- Simulators
- Tutorials
- Interactive games
- DVDs, television tuners

Vessel Administration
- Financial records
- Boat reference information, manuals etc
- Connect to engine instruments for alarms, service intervals etc

These applications can be broadly split into the six areas shown below, which are described in detail in the following chapters:

2   Chart Plotting and Automated Navigation

3   Tides and Traditional Navigation Aids

4   Communications

5   Weather Information

6   Vessel Administration

7   Training and Entertainment

Additionally, we will take a look at the Internet in chapter 8. Although it's not likely that the average yachtsman will currently be 'surfing the Internet' from on board, very many already connect to the Internet for e-mail via cellular 'phone or satcom links, and as satcoms get more affordable and faster, surfing from on board will also become commonplace.

Most importantly, though, there are a large number of resources available on the Internet which are of use to yachtsmen; 'Internet Cafés' are now so widespread, that taking your laptop ashore to visit supplier web sites, or weather sources for example, is now an extremely viable option.

The following chapters explore the six main types of marine software available. Where possible, the authors have avoided the use of trade or brand names, and readers should be aware that unless stated clearly as fact, statements made are solely the opinion of the authors.

Following this, the book provides some practical advice on choosing and installing a PC, interfacing it to your on-board instruments and discusses the merits of upgrading, rather than replacing your PC.

2 ■ Chart Plotting and Automated Navigation

Chart plotting, or electronic charting, is probably the biggest single reason for purchasing a PC for use on board. Most yachtsmen have a Global Positioning System (GPS) set and the addition of a PC and suitable software can give you an automatic chart plotting capability that may let you do more than the ECDIS systems used on board the largest merchant and naval vessels.

If you already own a suitable computer, then using a PC-based electronic charting system (ECS) provides an extremely low cost solution – usually far less than purchasing a dedicated colour chart plotter – whilst giving access to the highest quality navigational charts and very powerful navigation functions.

Note that as well as GPS receivers, most electronic charting systems will work with Loran and differential GPS (dGPS), as long as they can export latitude and longitude information in a format that the software can understand.

Even a simple laptop-based set-up can be very powerful

Choosing an electronic charting system

There is now a large choice of electronic charting software available and it can be tempting to rush into the process of choosing a system on the basis of one or two appealing features seen at a boat show presentation. Do bear in mind that some features are so important that they should be considered before all others. For example, even if a particular product has all the bells and whistles that you think you need, if it won't run on the operating system your computer uses, or does not have the chart coverage for the areas you sail in, it is obviously not worth considering.

One of the really important questions that should be addressed first is *chart compatibility*. Some chart plotting systems will only work with one brand of electronic chart, so if you have identified a system you are considering purchasing, check very carefully that charts are available for the area you are interested in, and that you are satisfied with the quality and detail of those charts.

Choosing a system therefore could perhaps be regarded as a back-to-front process, with the actual system features being compared after deciding which kind of electronic charts you wish to use. For this reason, we'll look at electronic charts first before investigating what electronic charting systems have to offer.

Choosing electronic charts

There are two main kinds of technology used in the manufacture of electronic charts; these are concerned with how the chart data itself is actually stored in the electronic chart. The two technologies are called raster and vector, and give each type of chart particular characteristics, which are discussed in the section below.

Raster charts

Nearly all raster charts are produced by feeding an original complete paper chart (or the printing films that were used to produce it) through a large-format digital scanner. This converts the chart information into a computer file comprised of a grid (a raster) of dots (or pixels – picture elements) of varying colour. The resulting computer file is then geo-referenced so it may be used with electronic charting software. Geo-referencing is simply providing information so that a real-world latitude and longitude position can be automatically converted to a position on the chart, and vice versa, allowing for any differences between the GPS and chart datum. Following geo-referencing, raster charts undergo a final quality assurance process and are then stored as computer files in a special format to help them load into the PC as quickly as possible.

Usually, raster chart files will also be encrypted to prevent illegal copying, or so they work only with certain electronic charting systems.

The chart is scanned at sufficiently high resolution, anything up to 250 dots per inch (dpi), so that in normal use, the user's eyes are fooled into seeing the complete chart image rather than the dots that comprise it. The drawback with scanning the chart at a very high resolution is that the chart files are large and take a long time to draw – a laptop PC screen has a resolution of about 70-80dpi.

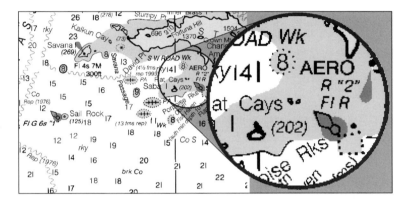

Like a newspaper photograph, a raster chart is comprised of a pattern of dots

Raster charts have the benefit that they appear on-screen exactly the same as the original paper version, and therefore navigators tend to have a high degree of confidence in them. They are also relatively quicker and cheaper to produce than vector charts, thus worldwide coverage is significant and growing fast. A drawback is that the chart files are quite large, and that although they may look good when viewed at their 'scanned-in' scale, when you zoom out to see more of the chart on the screen the quality of the image can deteriorate markedly. To minimise this, you should have charts covering a good range of scales, so the system can always display a chart at or close to the scale you require.

Vector charts

The technology used to create vector charts is more advanced than that used for raster charts. In a vector chart, each chart feature is stored as a mathematical vector describing its shape and size, rather than as a pattern of dots. They can be created in several different ways.

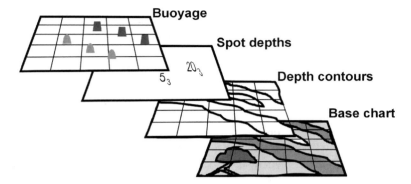

Buoyage

Spot depths

Depth contours

Base chart

Vector charts are actually made up of a series of layers

Firstly, they may be created by fixing a paper chart onto a 'digitising tablet'; this is a flat table which has a grid of electronic wires embedded in it. An operator moves an electronic 'puck' or cursor over the features on the chart, and the location of the puck is recorded by the network of wires. In this way, the location of every feature on the chart is translated by the digitising software into a vector database of the chart features.

Nowadays, very few vector charts are created using this old-fashioned method, which is quite slow and limited in accuracy. Many charts are now created using a 'head-up' digitising process. With head-up digitising, the paper or film original is scanned in much the same way as for a raster chart; the resulting raster computer file is then displayed on a PC screen, and an operator traces each chart feature using a pointer on-screen. This method is far more accurate than using a digitising tablet; it is also much faster, because the digitising software can perform specialised tasks such as semi-automatic line following.

Because experienced humans carry out both of these methods, it is possible to not only record the location of each feature, but also to group similar features together, or to include 'attributes' that further define each feature. Similar types of features may be stored on 'layers' and, by doing this, the chart can be said to include some form of 'intelligence'. For example, an electronic chart system could interrogate the vector chart to find the value of the nearest spot depth, or to provide further information on a navigational mark.

Currently, the vast majority of vector charts are created as described above. But already, the new generation of official vector charts are being produced by a combination of head-up digitising and 'direct data import'. Direct data import has become possible as an increasing amount of hydrographic survey data is captured and stored electronically – an electronic chart may now be produced completely electronically, with no paper being involved at all.

Hybrid charts   Another kind of electronic chart that may yet become more common is the hybrid chart. Essentially this is a combination of a raster chart with varying amounts of vector data added, as an 'intelligent underlay'. An attempt to overcome the limitations of raster charts, these allow private chart manufacturers 'add value' to charts for yachtsmen. They can offer the best of both worlds, by combining a clear, familiar looking raster chart with some of the intelligence of vector data, such as depths and contours, or navaid information, which may be displayed by suitable software.

So which is better, raster or vector?   This is a very common question from those who are new to electronic charting. The straight answer is that neither raster nor vector is inherently 'better' than the other type.

Certainly, raster charts include none of the intelligence of vector charts: they are a simple, flat picture, therefore vector charts are considered to be superior to raster. Experienced users of electronic charting systems almost always prefer using vector chart data, though navigators who are new to electronic charting may be happy to forgo the extra functionality of vector charts for the simplicity of raster charts.

For this reason, the reader who wishes to purchase an electronic charting system is advised to choose a system that lets them use both types. If not, then they should satisfy themselves as to which kind of electronic charts they prefer before making a purchase, as it is seldom possible to return electronic charts on the basis of preference. Changing your software and replacing all your raster charts with vector ones can prove expensive!

In conclusion, raster charts are familiar to the navigator because they appear identical to the paper charts from which they were scanned. They are also simple to use and no special knowledge or training is required to use them safely and effectively. Vector charts on the other hand are intelligent in that chart layers can be 'interrogated' by charting software eg querying depth contours. Also, their relatively small file size means they tend to display quickly and can give a clearer display than raster charts by allowing features to be shown sharply for each zoom level.

Other kinds of 'chart' data

Many navigators will readily appreciate the benefits of using an electronic facsimile of a paper chart on their PC, whether stored in a raster or vector format. But as so often happens with computing, the very technology employed makes it possible to do far more than just 'copy' the old, manual method.

The way that chart information is stored in a vector chart makes it possible to not only display that same data in different ways, but also to quite easily add detail to electronic charts that was not present on the original paper chart.

Bathymetric datasets

The design of vector charts makes them inherently able to represent the bathymetric (or depth) information they contain in a 3-dimensional format. However until recently, PC processor and graphics capabilities have not been up to the job of displaying this kind of information convincingly.

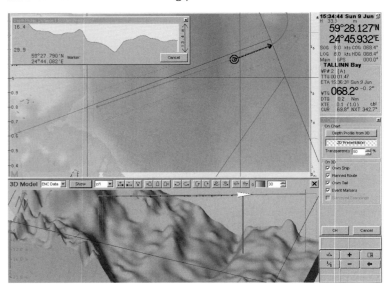

A useful display, combining 2-D and 3-D views and showing the vessel, her track and route

Now though, the kind of PC required to do this job is not the expensive, top of the range model, but the basic laptop or desktop machine you may already own.

As a result, many of the electronic charting system manufacturers have rushed to provide the facility to display this information in their programs. The displays look great – as these samples show –

Manufacturers show bathymetric data in different ways – which is most useful to you?

and though probably particularly useful for divers and fishermen, even yachtsmen find that this kind of representation helps them get a better 'feel' for the underlying seabed and spot hazards they may have missed on a normal chart.

So, having seen that existing chart information can be made more useful by displaying it in different ways, electronic chart and system manufacturers can also improve their offerings by including additional information from other sources. Again, the underlying georeferencing technology of vector charts makes this possible.

Almanac and pilotage information

Chart manufacturers can add 'hotspots' to their charts, linked to different kinds of information that is of use to the navigator.

This includes 'chartlets' taken from nautical almanacs, written pilotage notes and harbour information, even oblique aerial photography, illustrating anchorages or difficult approaches.

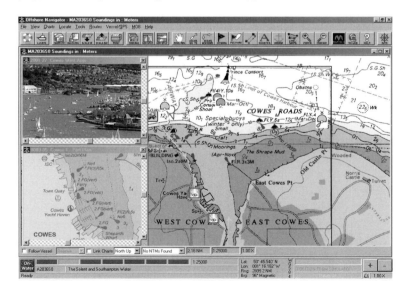

A basic raster chart with 'hotspots' added, linking to aerial photography and a harbour plan

Chart manufacturers

There is intense competition between the manufacturers of the various kinds of electronic charts currently available. This is not surprising because there is a lot of money to be made out of electronic charts in the years ahead. This is mainly from the commercial sector, so it's no surprise that it is their requirements, rather than those of leisure yachtsmen, that tend to be taken into account.

To show there's no preference from the authors, the companies are listed in strictly alphabetical order!

- **C-Map** (NT+ and CM/93) – This Italian company is probably the oldest existing manufacturer of vector charts, with a large collection of charts. Historically most of its charts were supplied on cartridges for use with dedicated plotters; however many PC-based systems use C-Map charts, on CD-ROM or using a cartridge reader that plugs into the PC. The NT+ format is aimed more at the leisure market, the CM/93 format for commercial users, offering more frequent updates, and a price structure more geared towards large chart folios. In both cases, chart are sold in folios with a variety of sizes available.

- **Euronav** (Livechart 'B') – These charts are digitised in England from paper charts and also created from digital data imported from hydrographic offices. The charts are sold either as single charts by chart number, or grouped into special value packs offering area coverage at a reduced cost. Coverage is best in Europe, the Mediterranean and the Caribbean. Commercial update contracts are available. The charts are primarily used in Euronav's seaPro system.

- **Mapmedia** – These raster charts are made by the French company Mapmedia, and are used primarily in Informatique et Mer's Maxsea chart plotter. They have excellent coverage in the Mediterranean, and are also faster to display than many other raster chart formats due to their database technology.

- **Maptech** (ChartPack/BSB, ChartKit, PhotoChart) – This American chart manufacturer has a long history of producing raster charts, originally as Resolution Mapping. Maptech is the official producer of NOAA charts for the US government and not surprisingly, initially coverage was US centric. But Maptech now offers good European coverage based on paper charts from many European hydrographic offices. The older ChartPack (PCX) format is less common than the ChartKit (BSB) format.

PhotoCharts are satellite photos, georeferenced so as to display on screen like charts.

- **Navionics** – Like C-Map, Navionics is one of the older vector chart producers. Until recently, almost all of its output was in cartridge form for dedicated plotters, but now some PC systems work with its 'Floppy Charts'.

- **Softchart** – A US company producing raster charts mainly based on US NOAA paper charts, though with a modified colour scheme.

- **Transas** (also marketed by Nobeltec as 'Passport Charts') – Transas offers a good worldwide catalogue of vector charts. Originally, much of its catalogue was based on Russian cartography; more recently, however, a greater proportion of its charts is based on UK Hydrographic Office paper charts.

- **UK Hydrographic Office** (ARCS) – The Admiralty Raster Charting Service (ARCS) offers most of the British Admiralty's range of paper charts in its own raster format. There are two levels of service: Navigator (a weekly updated service aimed at commercial users); and Skipper, aimed at the leisure user (where updates can be obtained quarterly). Some hydrographic offices (Australia, New Zealand and the Republic of South Africa) are producing charts in a format similar to ARCS, others (including the Netherlands) are having their charts produced in ARCS format by the UK Hydrographic Office.

Other electronic chart issues

Copyright

Carrying out accurate surveys of the seabed and preparing navigational charts is an incredibly expensive business, typically undertaken by governments rather than private organisations. Because of the high cost of production, chart manufacturers are understandably concerned about mariners making illegal copies of paper charts and are rigorous in enforcing copyright.

Although in certain parts of the world the practice of photocopying paper charts is quite widespread, providing chart data electronically makes it much more susceptible to illegal copying. For this reason, some producers of electronic charts employ some form of hardware copy protection to prevent illegal copying (see dongles, overleaf). A notable exception is for chart data produced by some American companies – many American electronic charts are royalty free and are freely copyable – though they are priced at such a low level that users prefer to buy rather than steal them.

Delivery formats

PC based charts are usually delivered on CD-ROM, and then either run from the CD or installed onto the PC's hard disk. Some manufacturers, such as C-Map, Euronav, Transas and the UKHO, provide their whole collection in an encrypted format on one or more free CD-ROMs; they then issue an 'unlock code' for the charts you want to purchase. This is very convenient when cruising, as you can often obtain unlock codes over the phone or via e-mail without needing to wait to have a new CD delivered.

C-Map and Navionics also issue charts on cartridges – charts are not installed onto the PC, but are read directly from the cartridge. Navionics uses the standard PC Card (PCMCIA) format. C-Map's NT+ cartridge format requires a special cartridge reader for the PC, but an advantage of this system is that the same chart cartridge can be used in your PC or in a dedicated plotter, so you always have a backup system.

Dongles

A 'dongle', or 'security key', is a small hardware device which is used by software manufacturers to prevent illegal copying of software and data. It is characterised by having a unique number and normally consists of a small amount of electronic circuitry and some memory. The whole lot is encased in plastic and fitted with a connector at one end that fits the PC and usually another connector to which a peripheral such as a printer may be connected.

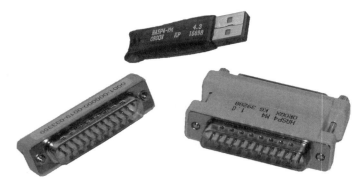

A selection of dongles. Note the low-profile parallel port type (left) and the USB type (top) compared to an older parallel port dongle (right)

At the most basic level, the software manufacturer designs his program so that while it is running, it periodically checks that a valid dongle is present. If not, the program will shut down.

More sophisticated dongles will have enough memory fitted so that the software manufacturer can store data in it – this may include 'permissions' to allow certain features of the software to operate, or permissions allowing particular electronic charts to be used.

In this way, even if an unscrupulous user makes an illegal copy of a program or data, as they can't replicate the dongle, they won't be able to use the stolen software or data.

Dongles are a very effective method of copy protection and are almost universally used by European electronic charting system manufacturers; however, yachtsmen feel vulnerable that if the dongle fails whilst at sea, they will not be able to use their program and charts. In fact, dongles are solid-state devices and, if treated with reasonable care, are extremely reliable; indeed some designs may last almost indefinitely.

It is worth pointing out, though, that since the dongle effectively represents the entire value of the software and data that require its presence, you should take care of it and insure it against all risks, just as you would with the PC you have it plugged into.

Manufacturers will almost certainly refuse to replace lost or stolen dongles, but may at their discretion, and for a fee, replace dongles returned to them which have been damaged by fire or water etc. Note the use of the phrase 'at their discretion' and do not be tempted to open the case of the dongle since any suggestion of tampering usually prevents a manufacturer from replacing a dongle.

Most dongles are designed to fit the computer's parallel (printer) port – you plug the dongle into the port on the PC, and a parallel port type printer plugs into the back of the dongle. Usually this works well, though some have had problems when using the dongle and the printer at the same time.

USB dongles (see also page 108) are becoming available which can circumvent these problems (and for those whose laptop does not have a parallel port), but because they are not 'pass-through' devices you lose a USB port.

Although they generally work very well, there are some problems associated with using dongles.

- Firstly, to function they require electrical power that they draw from the connector they are plugged into. Some users with very recent notebook computers have reported dongle problems, and it is suspected that in the quest for longer battery lives, some laptops fail to deliver sufficient electrical power to the dongle. If you experience this, it may be worth switching off any power-saving features on the PC (run the 'Power Options' program in the Control Panel).

- Although not usually a problem with desktop or Marine PCs, on laptops the dongle sticks out from the back of the PC and can be vulnerable to damage. Look for low-profile dongles, or purchase a flexible ribbon cable extension to let you tape the dongle to the back of the lid of the laptop.
- If your printer causes problems with your dongle, try temporarily disabling the printer driver software. You could also add a second printer port to a desktop PC, or it may be worth replacing a parallel type printer with a USB one.

Which GPS navigator?

Though some yachtsmen have sophisticated systems, with many different instruments interfaced together, the usual set-up is to have just a basic GPS navigator interfaced to the PC.

The navigator must be able to export data in the NMEA0183 format. Not all navigators are capable of this. Some of the cheapest hand-held units are simply unable to export data at all, while others that can are unable to do so unless connected to the boat's DC electrical supply by an optional cable.

Owners of 'networked' or 'integrated' instrument systems may discover that they need to buy an interface box to convert the manufacturer's own data language into NMEA0183 (see page 127).

While shopping around for a GPS, remember that most charting software can 'upload' lists of waypoints or routes to a suitable unit. This can be a very useful function, but check the GPS specifications carefully – not all units that export data can also import it.

Hand-held or fixed GPS sets are suitable, but check they 'speak' NMEA0183

Are paper charts still required?

The legal position is quite clear for large commercial vessels and, although less so for leisure vessels, it is important to note that electronic charts are not legal replacements for paper charts unless part of a system where the computer hardware, software and charts have all been 'type-approved' for navigation. Thus navigators should always carry up-to-date official charts, and consult them frequently.

Irrespective of the legal situation, it is undoubtedly poor seamanship to rely on just one means of position fixing, whatever it is, and it makes obvious commonsense to have a non-electronic back-up in case of power or equipment failure on board.

Many small craft navigators compromise, by using a PC-based electronic charting system as their primary navigation system, with a smaller number of smaller-scale paper charts as a back-up.

Chart datums

All of us who are used to navigating in tidal waters will be familiar with the term 'chart datum' – this term is often used to describe the depth of water over chart features at (usually) the Lowest Astronomical Tide (LAT), and Highest Astronomical Tide (HAT) for air gaps, in Europe. By taking the height of tide from local tide tables, and adding it to the charted depth over datum, we can quickly get an idea of how much water there actually is at a given point.

This 'chart datum' is actually the 'vertical datum', a reference or starting point from which heights and depths of various chart features are measured. It is not a geographically fixed datum, but rather varies locally – for example, as you sail up-river the vertical datum is moved up to match the rising river bed.

With GPS navigation and electronic charting however, the navigator is particularly concerned with horizontal datums. A horizontal datum is a model of the shape of the earth in the area covered by the chart, primarily concerned with the diameter of the earth and how far off spherical it is. Some datums such as WGS84 are global, whilst others are regional, for example the OSGB36 datum used around UK waters.

The use of the WGS84 datum is an essential part of the Global Positioning System, and all GPS receivers calculate their position in this datum. However, some paper charts (and therefore electronic charts) are referenced to datums other than WGS84, thus when plotting a position directly from a GPS set (that has been set to display WGS84) onto a non WGS84 paper chart, the position will probably be wrong. Around the UK, where the Ordnance Survey of Great Britain 1936 (OSGB36) or European Datum 1950 (ED50) datums are commonly used, the position error is generally less than 200 metres, but in some parts of the world errors of up to three miles have been reported.

In practice, the situation isn't as bad as it sounds, since for most of the common marine chart datums, fairly accurate offsets from WGS84 are known, or can be automatically worked out using polynomial calculations. These corrections may reduce the error to a few metres (depending upon the scale of the chart in question).

An electronic charting system may give the user the ability to apply these datum corrections automatically, not at all, or to use user-supplied corrections. With good-quality charts, where the position shift to the WGS84 datum is known accurately, the best option is to leave the GPS set outputting WGS84, and have the chart plotter correct this to the chart datum. This is because the processors in GPS receivers do not always have the computing space and power for accurate conversion between different datums.

> **Important Note** – Before GPS navigation became common, few navigators were aware of, or needed to know about, horizontal chart datums, because their navigation (at least in sight of land) tended to be *relative* to visible chart features. With the advent of *absolute* navigation, using highly accurate satellite-derived positions, small craft navigators should be aware that the charts (whether paper or electronic) they are using may not be as accurate as their position-fixing equipment. Therefore they should build in a suitable safety margin when planning passages or navigating. ***This is particularly important now that GPS accuracy has increased with Selective Availability (SA) having been switched off, or if using a differential GPS receiver (dGPS)***

Depth units

While the whole world is now officially 'metricated', many paper charts are still in print which are based on surveys carried out decades ago. Electronic charts taken from these paper charts will almost certainly use either feet or fathoms/feet as their depth units. Although new editions of these charts are usually metric, it will be some years before all charts are published using metric depths. **For this reason, the electronic charting system you choose should make it very clear to you which depth units are used by the chart you are viewing.**

Can I make my own charts?

There are some chart plotting products on the market that allow the user to scan in a portion of a paper navigational chart on a normal desktop scanning machine, and to display that on-screen. This concept is very appealing – generally speaking, once a navigator has purchased a paper chart, copyright law should not prevent him from scanning the chart *for personal use*, and using it with an electronic charting system.

A word of warning, however. The process by which paper charts are converted for use with computers is very involved. Correcting the scanned image for inaccuracies during the scanning process, 'warping' the scanned chart to match the correct map projection and correctly relating the electronic chart to a suitable geodetic datum, mean that an inexperienced user may have problems producing electronic charts that are consistently accurate enough for safe navigation.

Of course, the choice is yours, but if you wish to 'make your own electronic charts' as opposed to purchasing those created by experienced cartographic professionals, you should at least be aware of the possible sources of error and navigate accordingly.

Updating electronic charts

Most chart producers offer updated versions of their charts at a reduced cost. Although you need to contact the chart suppliers direct for accurate quotations, it is usually possible to update an electronic chart you have bought for around one quarter of the new price.

Beware of the difference between Notice to Mariner (NM) corrections and chart re-issues (or new editions) though: usually, as with paper charts, there comes a point where it is not possible for the manufacturer to keep a chart up-to-date just by applying NM corrections. When this happens, the manufacturer usually withdraws the original chart and re-issues another (often with the same chart number, but with a different edition or issue number). As with paper charts, this may mean that you have effectively got to buy the electronic chart again at its full price, although some chart manufacturers will supply new editions/re-issues at a reduced price.

Some manufacturers offer updating services, on a weekly, monthly or quarterly basis, where they manage your chart portfolio for you and automatically send you chart updates, as and when they become due. These services are really aimed at commercial navigators and, due to the open-ended nature of these services, may prove quite costly for the leisure yachtsman if the charts covered have had many changes.

Each chart manufacturer has a different policy towards providing updated charts to users and the electronic chart marketplace is changing very quickly, so after taking the general advice above into account, it is wise to get specific advice from an experienced supplier at time of purchase.

Chart rotation

Often, a navigator will find it more convenient to rotate a paper chart so that he is viewing it 'heading up' or 'course up' or 'leg up', as opposed to the more usual 'North up'. Research has shown that this is particularly useful when piloting in coastal waters, or when the chart is displayed beside a radar display. With raster charts it is not possible to rotate text so that it reads correctly whichever way up the chart is, but this is often possible with vector charting systems. If a vector system does rotate text, how is the rotation point handled, ie does the rotated text obscure the feature it is describing or other adjacent features? Ultimately, consider whether chart rotation actually enhances the usability of the chart.

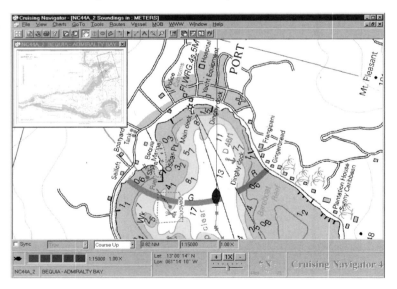

Chart rotation allows a charting system to mimic how a navigator may use paper charts in pilotage situations

Overzoom

The ability to 'overzoom' an electronic chart – that is, enlarge the image more than normal – can be very useful, especially on smaller PC displays using vector charts. It can allow you to examine chart details more closely, or can help if the display is hard to see. Do make sure, though, that an overzooming system will display a prominent warning when in overzoom mode. This is because it would be very dangerous to look at an overzoomed smaller scale chart, believing it to be as accurate and as detailed as a larger scale chart.

Choosing an electronic charting system

Having decided which kind of electronic charts you wish to use, you should have automatically narrowed down the choice of electronic charting systems. Now it is time to look at the different kinds of electronic charting system and to discover the kinds of things to look for when choosing between them.

Planning or plotting?

There are really two main kinds of electronic charting systems. Firstly, and probably most obviously, is that of chart plotting. This is the simplest type: it takes the vessel's position from a suitable navigator and displays it on top of an electronic chart 'backdrop'. Chart plotting software may also keep an electronic log book of the vessel's position and display the vessel's historical track on the chart as well. This is an incredibly useful function that allows the navigator to keep a constant, accurate plot at all times. Of course, chart plotting software may perform other functions as well, but all will be associated with displaying the vessel's current position etc.

Full electronic charting systems perform all of the plotting functions as described above, but allow you to plan passages as well. Although the benefits of ordinary chart plotting are clear to see, the extra functions provided by full electronic charting systems make these very powerful systems, often for a small incremental cost.

Using an electronic charting system with planning capability means that the navigator can build up routes from lists of waypoints. If the electronic charting system includes tidal stream information, it will usually allow you to calculate the effect of the tide on your route as well. Some systems even provide an 'optimisation' capability, ie tell you the best route to take for maximum advantage of the tidal stream, even ocean currents or the forecast weather.

Waypoint navigation

Historically, small boat navigators within sight of land both planned and plotted their voyages by referring to chart features in relative terms, eg one mile due south of Bolt Head. Relative navigation is second nature to most navigators, but does require charted features to be visible to be of any use: it can be very difficult to return to a particular spot at night or in poor visibility purely by dead reckoning, or without radar.

Since GPS receivers have become common on board small vessels, many navigators have become familiar with the concept of waypoint navigation. A waypoint is quite simply a shorthand notation for a location you have been to or may wish to go to. A waypoint has two elements: a name and a position (expressed as latitude and longitude). GPS receivers usually have the ability to store and recall a limited number of waypoints – this can be very useful when wishing to go to a particular location when visibility is poor. However, manipulating and using lots of waypoints can be challenging on the typical GPS receiver with a small screen and few buttons.

With PC-based systems, however, waypoint navigation really comes into its own. A large (often unlimited) number of waypoints with long, descriptive names may be stored on the PC's hard disk in different files and these waypoints can be easily built into routes, reversed, or replanned from your current position, ignoring waypoints already passed. Usually electronic charting systems are able to upload and download these waypoint lists to a suitable GPS receiver as well.

The following are all useful features that you might look out for when choosing an electronic charting system for your needs.

Multiple chart formats

As previously discussed, no one single electronic charting system has full worldwide coverage; therefore, to ensure widest possible coverage, it's important to purchase a system that can use more than one kind of electronic chart. This may not seem important if you usually cruise in just one area, but these days many people find themselves sailing further afield than they have expected, or go on charter holidays, where electronic chart coverage may differ from their home area.

It's wise to choose a system that lets you use raster charts and vector charts together so you can take advantage of the strengths of each type. For example, vector charts are particularly useful at smaller scales (say 1:100,000–1:1,000,000), where it is handy to be able to zoom in and out and to retain a clear chart display. Raster charts are most useful at scales of 1:75,000–1:20,000 and visually work very well for harbour approaches and plans.

Multiple chart windows

One of the main problems with electronic charting systems on board at the current time is that of display size. A typical laptop PC screen may measure just 12.1" to 15" in size and will have a resolution of 800x600 or 1024x768 pixels. Even if a charting program is able to zoom in and zoom out (and particularly with raster charts), this means that the program will not be able to clearly display all of the electronic chart at once. A useful solution is to be able to divide the screen up into one or more 'windows'. Each window may contain an image of the same chart (or a different one), zoomed in by different amounts, which will allow the navigator to see not only the detail around the vessel, but the *context* of the voyage as well.

All in all, multiple chart windows are extremely useful and this feature should be placed pretty high up on the list of desirable features. Incidentally, one might assume that dividing an already small screen up into smaller windows would make the system less useful, but in fact this is not the case because each window contains more *useful* information than would a single chart window.

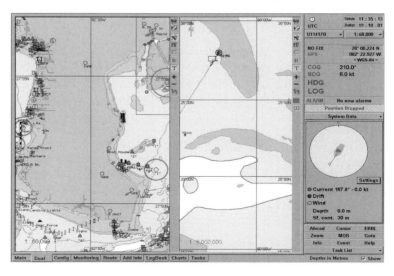

Multiple chart windows make good use of the available screen real-estate

Vessel following

Called by as many different names as there are manufacturers, this is a particularly useful feature whereby the system moves the electronic chart so as to keep the vessel symbol roughly centred on the chart. Some systems move the chart smoothly 'under' the vessel, others appear jerky and unnatural (especially on less powerful PCs). Many systems will change the chart automatically (or prompt you to load the next chart) when they reach the edge of the current chart in order to keep the vessel in view.

Look out for systems that let you change exactly *when* the chart scrolls and by how much; some systems 'look ahead' so you are viewing more of the chart in front of the vessel than behind. 'In front' is usually determined by the GPS course or compass heading.

For systems that offer multiple chart windows, check that it is possible to have some of them following the vessel and some of them not – that way, you can be planning this afternoon's passage in one window, whilst monitoring the current passage in another.

Autopilot control

Most chart plotting systems currently on the market claim to offer autopilot control as one of their features. Although the amount of control they offer varies between systems, usually they let you choose a course to steer on the PC and the system exports this to a suitable autopilot. Unless the autopilot is in standby mode, it should immediately try to bring the vessel round to the selected course. Some systems will automatically instruct the autopilot to change course once a waypoint is reached (or at least when the vessel gets within a user-selected distance from the waypoint).

> **Important Note** – Autopilot control is a very useful function, though it must be stressed that a good lookout should be kept at all times – it would be very dangerous to rely solely on an autopilot, especially in crowded waters or close to hazards.

Bearing and distance calculation

When navigating using paper charts, distances are usually measured off the vertical scale on the chart using a pair of dividers. This is not possible with electronic charting systems because of the way charts are displayed on-screen, so even the most basic system should provide measuring or 'A2B' tools which will let you determine the distance between two points.

More advanced systems will also display the bearing and the reciprocal between two points or allow you to quickly measure between several points at once. Some will even display measured distances according to rhumb line or great circle methods.

Routes

Virtually all systems allow you to build routes from the program's internal database(s) of waypoints, or by placing them graphically onto the chart with the mouse cursor. A route is simply a named list of waypoints, but look out for useful features such as the ability to reverse a route, or make a quick route from the vessel's current position. You should be allowed to annotate each route file and be able to save, copy, rename and delete them without having to leave the program. If it is important to you, look out for the ability to upload a complete route into a GPS, which can provide a useful back-up should your PC fail while at sea.

Passage planning and weather routeing

With the exception of basic systems, electronic charting programs will allow you to calculate the effect of external factors such as tides, currents and the weather on your intended route. It works like this: choose a series of waypoints to define your intended route, then choose a date and time of departure and a realistic vessel speed. Working from the PC's internal clock and relevant information supplied with your system, it will apply the effect of these factors on your route and display not only the expected time of arrival, but also an expected ground track. More advanced systems may also allow you to work 'backwards' and find out the best time to leave to take maximum advantage of at least the tides.

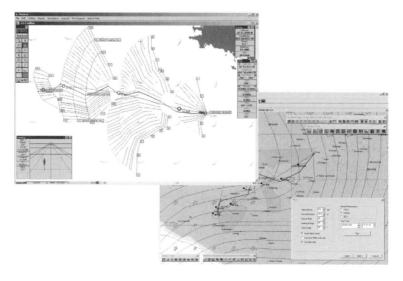

Often systems can help you plan passages taking into account tidal streams, ocean currents, even the weather forecast

Of course, we rarely sail to planned speed and sailing boats often can't make the desired course, so the ability to easily re-plan the rest of the route from your current position is useful. Being able to choose different speeds and allow leeway factors for each leg is also helpful for sailing boats.

There are so many variables affecting a small boat at sea that it would be unreasonable to expect these passage plans to be really accurate. However, the more accurate they are the better, so consider the quality and coverage of any included data. Some programs include ocean current and tidal stream data free of charge, but for a limited area – if you sail outside of this area, how will you obtain more data? Can you purchase a disk or must you type the data in? If the system works with weather forecasts, how will you access and download this information while at sea?

Some manufacturers advertise their system's ability to perform tidal passage planning, but don't actually include any data; remember to cost this in when you are comparing systems from different manufacturers. Also consider that some systems require an annual update to the tidal information, without which the tidal functions either won't work, or may be much less accurate.

Finally, consider where the data comes from in the first place. Private organisations as well as hydrographic offices provide tidal stream data; some is produced using mathematical models rather than observations. Weather information and ocean currents will also be mathematically modelled from a variety of original sources. This is one area where it will really pay to do some solid research before deciding on a system.

Tidal heights

Many programs come with a tides module that will work out times and heights of high and low water in various places (see next chapter). Whilst these are very useful pieces of software in their own right, it is even more convenient when built in to an electronic charting system. In any case, if the charting system is able to perform passage planning using tidal streams, it is very easy for the manufacturer to provide a tidal height function as well.

Dead reckoning

Since a chart plotting system by definition requires an electronic navigator input, it may seem odd to include a dead reckoning (DR) facility. The main reason this is important is if your navigator or its antenna should fail or if for some other reason the charting system detects that a valid GPS signal is not available to it.

A DR mode should allow you to choose a vessel location, course and speed and display the vessel symbol as if a GPS were connected. Provision of this useful facility varies between systems – some don't provide it at all; some do, but charge extra for it; and some include it as standard.

> **Important Note** – If the system you are considering does offer a DR facility, check whether it is automatically activated should the GPS fail. If so, it is *absolutely essential* that the system makes it very obvious it is operating in DR mode. The danger of course is that an automatic DR mode won't take into account actual course and speed changes and could therefore be showing the vessel in the wrong position.

Manual plotting

In case your GPS does fail, far more important than a DR facility is the ability to lay down observed bearings onto the electronic chart and to add a manually entered position within the resulting 'cocked hat'. It may also be desirable to be able to plot a line of position (LOP) derived from astro navigation. This manual log entry should have a manual 'time stamp' and it should be possible to expand on it with narrative text.

Look out for manual plotting tools that give you range and bearings from and to objects, that allow you to work in degrees true or magnetic and, above all, that are easy to use – if they're unfriendly, you won't play with them; if you don't play with them, you won't know how to operate them when you need to.

Man overboard

There are two schools of thought when it comes to man overboard (MOB) features on electronic charting systems. The first is that it is a very useful feature that may help to save life; the second is that the last thing anyone should be doing in a man overboard scenario is trying to remember how to activate the charting system's man overboard function.

Clearly both schools have their merit, but to help you decide whether this is important for you, try to follow the procedure through should you ever find yourself in this situation. If the charting system makes it **very easy** to record a MOB position (can it be connected to an MOB button in the cockpit?) and **automatically** provides **useful** information to help return to the casualty's last known position, it may be considered worthwhile, as long as all on board are fully trained in its use. If not, it simply isn't worth considering.

Some charting systems provide automatic search pattern generation which could be useful when planning an extended search and
rescue operation; however, in the authors' opinion there has yet to
be designed a simple and useful system that really offers more than
the MOB button found on most GPS receivers.

Logging

Basic chart plotting programs simply display incoming NMEA0183
data such as the vessel's position. More advanced systems are able
to save this data into a log file as well. If logging is important to you
(maybe for race analysis), look out for systems that will also allow
you to log other data – for example, true and apparent wind, depth
and water temperature etc. The best systems allow you to choose
the frequency with which data is written to the log file – this is
important because logged NMEA0183 data can quickly build up
into very large files on your PC's hard disk. Is the logging frequency
the same for every incoming data item or can you record each
type of data at different frequencies?

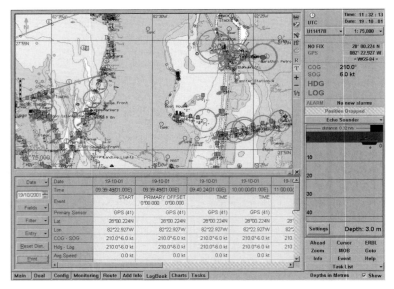

*Systems should
be able to clearly
log and display
information
relating to the
vessel and the
environment*

Simply logging incoming instrument data is all very well, but to be
of any use the log must also allow the navigator to add manual,
narrative log entries.

One other very useful function is the ability to play back the log of
a particular voyage or to display a previous voyage track if you
wish to retrace your steps.

Log graphing

Log graphing allows you to see incoming NMEA0183 data graphically. This is particularly useful for performance sailing where you can compare two or more parameters together, which makes it far easier to spot trends as they happen. Examples might be wind shifts or poor helming affecting the course or speed.

As well as being able to display incoming data in real-time, it can also be very useful to graph data off-line for performance analysis. The more powerful systems allow you to load up a previously recorded log file and to display the data in graph form. Some systems allow you to choose different graph types to help visualise different kinds of data more easily.

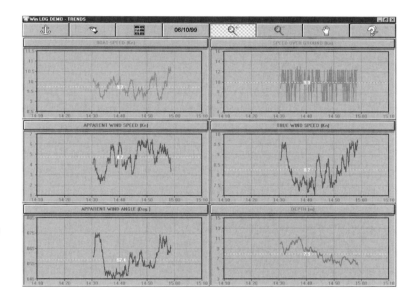

Graphing data is very useful for performance analysis

Overlaying data

Only the most basic electronic charting systems don't let you 'draw' on the electronic chart. The ability to mark areas to avoid, or to clearly mark dangers, is almost essential in a system to be used on board. Some systems have simple and easy to use 'freehand' drawing ability, whilst others offer comprehensive but much more complex line, arc, point and polygon drawing tools, even using multiple layers as in a graphics program. Look out for the ability to save and load your overlay files to disk, acquaint yourself with the user interface – even if the overlay function is powerful, if it's difficult to use, then you'll avoid using it.

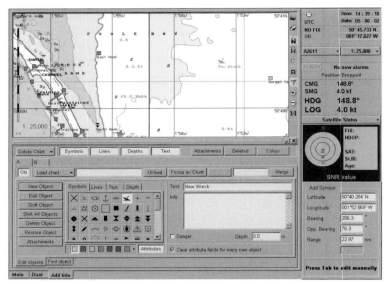

Overlays allow you to mark your own point, line and area information on the chart

One very popular use of overlay functions is the ability to build up your own pilotage notes. Text, scanned-in pictures, even video sequences, may be attached to 'hotspots' overlaid onto the electronic chart. When queried (usually by pointing at the hotspot and clicking with the mouse), the system should pop up a box showing the stored text, with buttons to view any attached pictures or video files. One of the most difficult things in the past was adding pictures to the system, but today's digital cameras and camcorders make this really easy.

Alarm zones

Several of the electronic charting systems currently available allow the user to add one or more alarm zones to the chart. This involves drawing an area (or, in simple systems, a circle) which, when the vessel enters or leaves it, triggers an alarm condition. Depending upon the system, the alarm may simply involve the display of a flashing button, or may use the PC's sound card to play an audible alarm. Bear in mind that unless you have powerful speakers attached to your PC (that are switched on!), an audible alarm may be difficult to hear over background noises, so rely on this feature with caution and make sure that the system provides a really noticeable visual alarm as well.

Now good quality vector data is more widespread, it is becoming viable to let your charting system generate certain types of alarm zone for you automatically. Some systems can generate a safe contour alarm, based on a safe depth you enter into the program at the start of your voyage, or during the planning process. Good systems should only make this feature available when using larger-scale charts, as it would be unwise to rely on a safe contour automatically generated using sparse information from small-scale charts.

A compromise may be to let the system highlight all depths shallower than 6 metres (for example) and then to use the system's alarm zone drawing tools to draw in your own alarm boundaries.

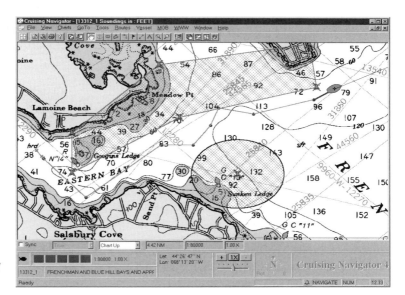

Alarm zones can be set to activate when the vessel enters or leaves them and should present visual and audible warnings

Radar and ARPA radar overlay

ARPA stands for Automated Radar Plotting Aid and until fairly recently, these radar sets were the preserve of commercial vessels only; however, a steady reduction in cost means that ARPA or Mini ARPA (MARPA) radars have become relatively common in the 11 metre (35 feet) and upwards bracket. In a traditional radar set, transmitted signals are bounced back to the vessel and are shown on the radar display as a series of blips. ARPA radars include powerful software that analyses patterns in the returned blips and highlights them as 'targets'. With a GPS set or an accurate log and heading sensor connected, the ARPA radar software is able to cancel out own vessel movement and highlight targets that are moving relative to the vessel and to the land. An ARPA radar set applies identification numbers to each target and some models are able to export these via NMEA0183. Along with the target vessel's identifier number, its position, course and speed, an ARPA radar may also export useful collision-avoidance information for each target, such as the closest point of approach and the time to it.

Recently, dedicated PC radar packages have appeared, incorporating a scanner head, electronics drivers and a computer interface card. Designed to replace the standalone radar, it displays the scanned radar image overlaid onto an electronic chart, or on its own. Others supply an interface unit that connects the output of a standard radar scanner to your PC. There is now a choice of several good quality systems that offer these features.

Night vision

Many system manufacturers claim to offer night vision capabilities. This is usually a choice of 'day', 'dusk' and 'night' settings, with the latter changing the colours of the display so as not to damage a navigator's night vision. Generally these work well, but do check that the system actually dims the Windows 'system colours' as well as just the chart window, since if not, the surrounding brightness can negate the usefulness of dimming just the chart display.

Performance sailing functions

Sailing boat navigators, particularly race boat navigators, have a number of specific extra requirements. Programs offering these functions have been available for use by competitors in events such as the *America's Cup*, *Volvo*, *Vendee Globe* and *Admiral's Cup*, but are now becoming available in more mainstream programs.

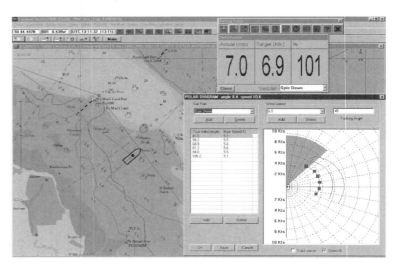

A boat's polar table(s) let the navigator know how well the boat is doing against her optimum performance

The key factors are concerned with boats sailing at different speeds on different points of sail, and of course not being able to sail directly into the wind. The program will have a model of the boat's performance, her polars, and use this to predict the speed on each leg, tacking and gybing laylines into the mark, and sometimes even the fastest route to the next waypoint. More sophisticated programs will also allow the navigator to monitor performance, and to experiment with different wind conditions.

Of obvious use for racing sailors, polars can also be useful for cruising yachtsmen – when we are sailing, how confident are we that we are doing as well as could be, or should be, for the conditions?

Fuel calculations

Tidal passage planning is certainly less important for semi-displacement/planing powered craft than it is for sailing boats, but some electronic charting systems will work out fuel consumption as well. The power boat owner types in the vessel's fuel consumption characteristics and this, together with the fuel cost per litre, lets him quickly work out the cost of a particular trip and so allows him to save money by working the tides to his advantage.

Interfacing

When evaluating systems, consider how well the software system copes with interfacing to a navigator and other on board instruments. Some systems will simply take NMEA0183 position information for plotting, others will 'understand' and use a wide variety of types of data, and some will even export or repeat data for other instruments (such as an autopilot or a radar) to use. Even if a system copes with a wide variety of data types, you should also consider how easy it is to set it up – this is an area that can be fraught with difficulties if the software you are using is 'unfriendly'. There are systems on the market that not only have comprehensive interfacing controls, but are also simple to set up, even being provided with tools to automatically analyse incoming data and to suggest an optimum set-up.

One thing is certain, most interfacing problems are caused by poor quality electrical connections between the 'talker' (eg GPS set) and the 'listener' (eg the PC's serial port). More information on this is to be found in chapter 11; success is largely in your hands, but it's worth pointing out that some system manufacturers supply a 'plain' serial cable, whereas others provide a proper shielded opto-isolated interface cable. The latter costs a bit more to provide, but nine times out of ten will solve physical interfacing problems that may be experienced with a plain serial cable.

Above, we refer to cables in the singular – in fact, you will usually have to deal with two cables, since most smaller GPS sets are fitted with proprietary connectors. Unless you have a suitable connector to plug into the GPS set, you will need to buy the manufacturer's own cable (often this same cable is used to get 12VDC power from the boat's supply). You connect the GPS cable's signal wires to those of the charting system's cable. Most manufacturers supply sufficient information for you to do this yourself, but you must make good connections – you *can* use 'chocolate block' type connectors, but as with all marine electrical connections, you are advised to solder and seal the connections for trouble-free operation.

In summary

The aforementioned points are really only scratching the surface with modern electronic charting systems. There are clearly many factors that may influence your decision as to which product to purchase, and as systems develop and manufacturers become more competitive, this process will get more complicated.

We have seen that it is best to decide on what kinds of charts you wish to use first, and to look at the features of the electronic charting system itself later. The real message has to be that you must 'try before you buy' since each system has differing user interfaces as well as capabilities. To this end, most manufacturers provide demonstration CD-ROMs which you can install on your PC and evaluate the system at your leisure. Better still, book a training session with a marine computing specialist, where you will be able to try several systems as well as pick the brains of experienced and impartial professionals.

3 ■ Tides and Traditional Navigation Aids

Although to many yachtsmen computer navigation is synonymous with electronic charting, there are other areas where computer power is useful in assisting traditional navigation techniques, without going over completely to electronic charting. Examples worthy of mention are tide height prediction and astro navigation programs. You may also consider using an 'electronic almanac' that replicates the information found in traditional paper publications, using the PC's multimedia capabilities to present the information in a format that is easy to access and understand.

Tide height prediction

Whether or not you take your PC on board, a tide height prediction program can make life so much easier, and the computerised version can work out cheaper than buying tide tables each year.

Simply select the location you want the tidal data for, and the range of dates, to bring up a graphical or tabulated tidal curve. It is very simple to identify the tidal height for a given date and time, or to

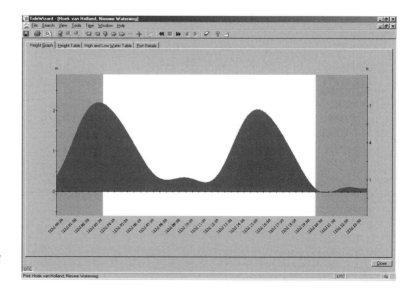

Tide height prediction programs are usually based on the same data as is used in printed almanacs

work the other way round and to find out at what time a required tidal height occurs.

Several of the programs currently available have a perpetual almanac and provide reasonably accurate calculations until the year 2100. Some programs also allow you to enter your boat's draft and mast height, together with charted depths and air clearances, and so can calculate clearance times for bridges and underwater obstructions.

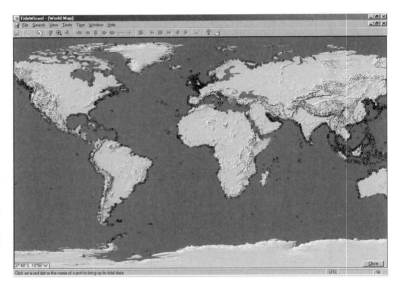

Many tide programs can give access to tidal height information covering over 4,500 primary and secondary ports worldwide

Too good to be true?

The big problem in predicting tides is that the heights are very dependent on atmospheric conditions, local geography, river flows etc. These factors have such a great effect on the actual amount of water available at a given time that all tidal height predictions (whether computer-based or tabulated in a printed almanac) should only be taken as a guide. Indeed, a purely theoretical/mathematical approach cannot be used. Additionally, tide heights are monitored over a period of time – ideally a full year but often a matter of weeks or days – and predictions are based on analyses of these observations.

One of the most obvious factors affecting tidal height is the wind – in time a wind will move water from the windward to the leeward shore. Barometric pressure also has a significant effect – an increase in pressure will reduce the height of tide. In a river, heavy rainfall upstream will work its way down the river, resulting in raised water levels. On a larger scale, some shallow confined seas, such as the North Sea, can have storm surges when the right combination of weather conditions occur.

There are a number of methods of predicting tides: in most waters, **harmonic analysis** gives the best results. Here various cyclical astronomical coefficients are modelled by a number of factors. Each factor has a cyclical period; and a time lag and amplitude, derived from observations. Astronomical coefficients vary in period from about 4 hours to 19 years.

In some waters, such as shallow estuaries, a standing wave can be set up in the estuary, causing further oscillations in tide heights. In the harmonic method this is modelled by a number of shallow water coefficients. However, in extreme cases, such as in some German waters, better results are obtained by using non-harmonic prediction methods.

The **Simplified Harmonic Method** (SHM) is an approximation of the Full Harmonic Method (FHM) that makes calculations much quicker with a relatively minor reduction in accuracy. It takes the groups of similar coefficients and consolidates them into four main coefficients, adjusted for astronomical factors. It also includes shallow water effects, and monthly seasonal variations in sea level and coefficients.

In printed tide tables, there are usually a small number of **primary ports** with pre-computed heights, where generally there has been at least a year's observations, and **secondary ports**. For each secondary port, a primary port with a similar tidal curve is selected as a base, and then time and height corrections are given relative to the primary port. This is a convenience for the navigator without a PC, and the results are generally less accurate than using the SHM.

Most tide prediction programs are based on the SHM, which is mostly accurate to about 0.1 metres for primary ports. Some PC programs or those for hand-held computers may use a reduced set of coefficients, and so be less accurate.

Other programs use the **Full Harmonic Method** (FHM), which offers greater theoretical accuracy than the SHM. In addition to the four primary factors, these systems may use over a hundred secondary factors for some locations (many of these may have only a minimal effect on the accuracy of the predictions). However, when one considers the additional cost of the data FHM systems require and all the external sources of inaccuracy – wind

strength and direction, atmospheric pressure, river flow and so on –
these systems are seldom recommended for normal leisure use.

Tidal passage planning

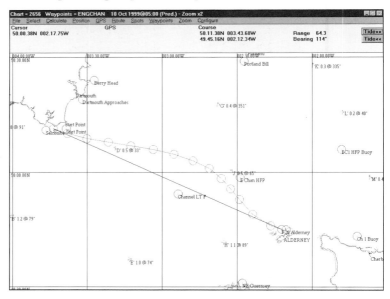

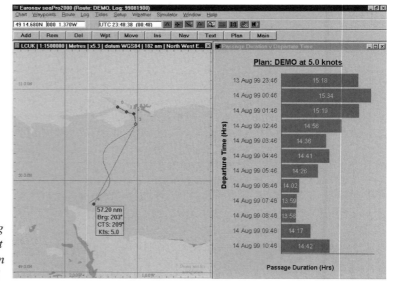

A simple, low-cost program (above right) can offer some of the advanced tidal passage planning capability of full electronic charting systems (right), but may run happily on a less powerful PC

Though many yachtsmen would like to run a full-blown electronic charting system on their PC, there are also those who prefer not to take a newer or more powerful PC on board; indeed, there are still many older PCs in regular use on board that are not powerful enough to run today's operating systems and electronic charting software. Some yachtsmen even argue that since they have a built-in dedicated chart plotter on their boat, they have no need for PC style high-quality electronic charts, but would still like a hand with tidal passage planning and don't see why they should pay the premium for the latest, high powered electronic charting system.

Fortunately, there is software available that was designed to run on older, less powerful computers. This software will perform simple tidal passage planning and optimisation functions, even displaying an expected ground track for a given boat speed and departure time. Even if not used on board, such a system will allow the navigator to print out a succinct plan of their route before going to sea. Some of these systems will also perform positional plotting from a GPS set whilst at sea, albeit on very basic, simplified charts.

Electronic almanacs

Though at the time of writing, there has yet to be a commercially successful electronic almanac produced, prototypes have been developed that show how the bulky and awkward tabulated information commonly found in a printed almanac can be combined into a consistent user interface on the PC, making it much more easy and convenient to use.

This idea certainly has appeal and could be immensely useful on board, as well as at home prior to going to sea. We mention this kind of product because it is likely that during the life of this book, such a program will be released.

An electronic almanac could include an enormous range of functions and information sources, including chart plotting and logging, tidal heights and streams, pilotage notes and weather and radio information. If it is well designed, so it is easy to find the desired information, this will be a very useful utility; more so if it elegantly interfaces to a chart plotting system.

Bear in mind that there will probably be ongoing costs associated with an electronic almanac – it would probably be purchased containing information for just one region or area, and if you wished to use it in a different area, you would need to purchase add-on area information. Similarly, much of the information found in a program like this must be considered perishable and would almost certainly need updating annually, if not more frequently.

Virtual pilotage

Many will be familiar with the sophisticated virtual 'walk-through' or 'fly-through' presentations often shown on TV documentaries – these are often used to demonstrate how a new building, an airport for example, will look once it has been constructed.

Now imagine being able to do the same with this summer's cruising destination on your PC. Virtual pilotage software is available for some areas which does exactly that. You plan your passage using simple electronic charts built-into the system, and then watch as the virtual pilotage software generates an incredibly detailed three dimensional representation of your cruising ground. Look up, down, astern, as you cruise around.

Not only is the surrounding landscape 'modelled' in these systems, things like navigation lights are portrayed realistically, and some even show the effect of the rising and falling tide, so as well as being fun to use, these systems can be really useful in familiarising yourself with a cruising area before you even get there.

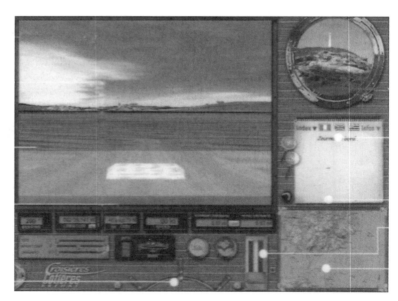

Virtual pilotage software can generate an uncannily lifelike representation of many cruising grounds

Astro navigation

Whilst almost everyone uses GPS as a primary means of navigation, for those who venture offshore it is still useful to be able to revert to astro when required, to safeguard against a damaged GPS receiver/antenna or poor signal reception. It is worth mentioning that GPS signals can be inadvertently jammed by sources such as TV transmitters, as well as intentional jamming tests occasionally carried out by the military. And for many there is just the pleasure of mastering a traditional method of navigation.

The drawback for many lies not so much in the use of the sextant, but in the volumes of tables and multitude of arithmetical operations needed to obtain a line of position (LOP). Though not difficult, there are many stages involved in obtaining an accurate LOP, and unless one regularly practises the procedure, it is very easy to make errors that will render the LOP hopelessly inaccurate.

Using a sight reduction program on the PC can make life much easier. Some, such as *Win Astro*, run on a PC, but others run on palm top devices. In all cases, though, their operation is similar.

Most systems let you enter an assumed position and your vessel's course and speed to give a dead reckoning (DR) position. Choose the celestial bodies to use and the program uses its built-in almanac to give you an approximate altitude (height) and azimuth (bearing) of the body. Set your sextant to the altitude and point it along the azimuth and you should see your chosen body.

Most programs contain extensive ephemera – details of all the heavenly bodies that are commonly used in astro navigation

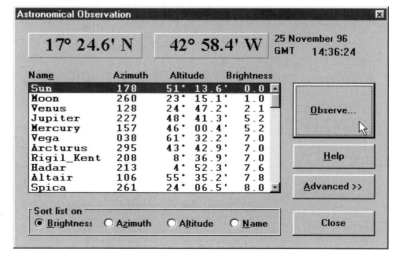

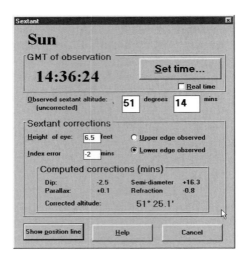

*The navigator
enters observed
data into a 'form';
the computer uses
this information to
produce a line of
position*

Once you have found the body, you take the actual sight(s) and
enter the GMT time and sextant altitude into a software 'form' on
your PC.

The software will then generate a line of position for you and give
you coordinates for a manual plot. No more messing about with
tables, and the result is available in just seconds.

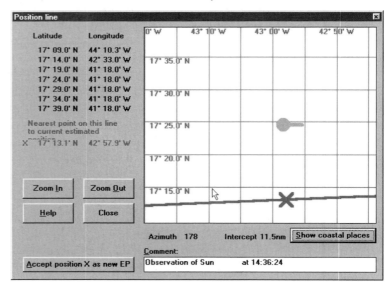

*A line of position
is easily plotted by
the computer from
its built-in
ephemera and the
navigator's
sextant sight*

One of the main pleasures of boating has to be 'getting away from it all'. For others, though, it is very important to be able to keep in touch with work or loved ones whilst away sailing. Increasingly, as powerful communications technologies have become much more affordable and reliable, many of us can justify spending more time on the boat because we can keep in touch with the office. Indeed, it is not unknown nowadays for an individual to be able to run a business entirely from on board their boat.

Spoilt for choice

Whilst not so many years ago mariners were limited to using fairly short range radio communications for voice contact with the shore, now there is a bewildering choice of radio, mobile phone, and satellite systems for use at sea, as well as the opportunity to connect your laptop PC directly to the terrestrial telephone network when ashore in many parts of the world. Each of these has its benefits, and there is no single perfect answer so many people end up using a mixture of more than one system.

Technically, all the systems discussed (except a direct connection to a land telephone line) rely on the same basic radio technology, but in view of the mixture of frequencies, ranges etc., we have for convenience divided this chapter into four parts. We briefly cover land lines, then look in more detail at cellular mobile phones, radio-based systems and finally satellite systems, present and future.

Land lines

Marina facilities

Marinas in the Mediterranean and the USA (and increasingly in Northern Europe and the Caribbean), provide a phone line that goes through the marina's exchange. For phone calls, this usually works out much cheaper than a mobile or satellite phone, but will also give you a much faster data rate (about the same as from a land line at home), making it really useful for e-mail and web access. It is worth keeping a domestic phone and a standard modem on board (if your laptop doesn't have one built-in) to use this facility when available.

Some marinas have installed local wireless networks for data access. This consists of a small antenna and receiver which you connect to your PC (via a PC Card or USB port) for the duration of your stay. Though a marina staff member will probably need to set this system up for you on your PC, it gives a much higher speed data connection than you would get via a normal land line.

Other shoreside facilities

For the sailor equipped with a laptop PC, there are plenty of choices for data communications. As well as the more obvious cybercafés (many of which will let you use your own laptop), the author has connected at harbour offices, restaurants, post offices, hotels, even a Turkish carpet shop! See pages 92-94 for more detail on getting online while ashore.

GSM mobile phones

Whether they call them cellphones, mobile phones or portables, most yachtsmen carry a GSM mobile phone on board for use as a telephone, and many will also link it to a PC for fax and data purposes. A big benefit of the GSM network is that it offers seamless 'roaming' between various countries in Europe, Asia and much of the USA, at time of writing, 181 countries in total – refer to the web site **www.gsm.org** for up-to-date coverage details. Most of the airtime providers have roaming agreements, letting you use your phone on other networks (there is a price premium for this). Bear in mind that though the GSM system itself allows seamless roaming, the underlying radio frequencies used in a country may vary.

In Europe the GSM networks use 900 and 1800MHz, and most phones support both frequencies; in North and South America they use 1900MHz. Thus you may need to purchase a tri-band phone if you want to use GSM in all these areas.

GSM coverage in the south of the UK from one provider, Vodafone, at time of writing

Coverage in the more developed parts of the world, particularly Europe, is excellent, but in more remote places may be patchy, though improving.

Mobile phone range is currently limited to about 20 miles offshore. You can improve this by having an external GSM antenna installed, preferably high up, with good quality antenna cable connecting it to the phone. Also some car and fixed phones transmit at a higher power than hand held phones, giving increased range and making the phone less likely to drop out when connected.

As an alternative to a hand held phone, you could use a fixed GSM unit, which will have a socket for connecting to a normal phone handset or (for bigger boats) a phone exchange; a serial port for data and fax communications; and sometimes an additional phone socket for a paper fax machine. This allows you to have more than one phone handset attached to the phone (for example in the saloon and the main cabin), or to have a DECT cordless phone.

If linking the phone to a PC, the standard GSM data rate is 9.6kbps, which is good for e-mail but a bit slow for web access. However the new General Packet Radio Service (GPRS) technology gives data rates of 30kbps, which is not much less than a normal dial-up modem. GPRS will also offer 'always-on' service, Internet-based content, colour Internet browsing, multimedia messages and location-based services

For PC users, the best thing about GPRS is that you pay for the volume of data and not the time connected, which makes it ideal for web browsing as you are not paying while you read the web pages, or whilst waiting for a download from a busy web site. To use GPRS you will need a GPRS capable phone plus a separate GPRS contract.

New developments in GSM technology will offer advanced mobile services such as the downloading of video and music clips, full multimedia messaging, high-speed colour Internet access and e-mail on the move. Attempts are also being made to offer better and faster services to users by improved co-ordination of the underlying technologies which provide the GSM service.

The main drawback with mobile phones is the cost of calling when roaming abroad, usually this is much higher than in the user's own country. Also, when receiving calls abroad, you will be charged for the roaming part of the call. These charges can vary enormously, so check your contract and be careful when you select which network to use when roaming. Alternatively if you will be staying in a country for a while, it can pay to get a 'pay as you go' phone locally, and use this for dialling-up and sending faxes.

Mayday! — A word of caution about mobile phones

Since the first Mayday message in the days of the *RMS Titanic*, maritime safety communications have been achieved by shore stations and vessels keeping a listening radio watch on specific radio channels. General voice communications or 'public correspondence' have also been achieved by linking these radio channels onto the public telephone network via shore stations.

Since the Global Maritime Distress and Safety System (GMDSS) was introduced in 1999, many vessels and coast radio stations are no longer obliged to keep a listening watch on the old safety channels. Instead safety messages are handled automatically by the GMDSS, using Digital Selective Calling (DSC) operating over VHF, MF, HF radio channels and via satellite systems.

Even before the GMDSS, yachtsmen discovered that mobile phones offered cheaper and more convenient communications than using 'link calls' to shore radio stations. Some yachtsmen ventured to sea without VHF radios and inevitably cellphones were used to summon emergency services. With improvements in mobile phone services and cheap satellite communications systems becoming available it is obvious that the temptation will be to ignore the official GMDSS system and to rely on other systems.

The authors stress that although using non-official communications systems to summon help *might* work, it cannot be guaranteed to do so. Therefore, whether required to by the GMDSS or not, ALL vessels should be fitted with GMDSS communications equipment appropriate to the area they will be operating in, in addition to any commercial communications system they may desire.

Non-GSM mobile phones

Though the GSM network is widely available worldwide, in the majority of the USA and the Caribbean, cellular phones operate on systems that do not work with GSM. In these areas, you will need to either buy or rent a phone and take out an airtime contract – but check with the service provider that the system supports data calls – not all do.

Fortunately for those cruising in the Caribbean, the French and Dutch islands are strategically located and do offer GSM service, so if you don't need to dial-up every day, it may suit you to wait until you cruise into an area with a GSM signal.

Radio-based data communication

Marine SSB radio

Not so long ago, the ONLY way of communicating between vessels or with the shore when more than a few miles off the coast was by single side-band (SSB) radio. By using a 'telex over radio' modem, it was possible for yachtsmen to use their SSB radio to send and receive telex messages. In the mid 1990s, 'gateways' were developed which allowed yachtsmen to have their telex messages automatically routed as e-mails onto the growing Internet.

The advent of low-cost satellite communications inevitably affected SSB's popularity, but it does seem to be making a comeback for voice communication – vessel-to-vessel communication is free and there are still a few coast radio stations that can link you in to the land telephone network if you wish to do this.

For data communication though, SSB has been effectively superseded by satellite communications. A couple of providers do offer e-mail and ftp services – however data rates are pretty slow at about 0.1kbps and operators such as Globe Wireless claim not to be attracting business from yachtsmen, instead concentrating on commercial markets. Though running costs are low, yachtsmen will need a radio modem for data communication and this can cost almost as much to buy as an Inmarsat C unit.

In the authors' view, probably the main benefit to today's cruising yachtsman of having an SSB transceiver on board is that as well as being used for voice communication, it can also double as a receiver for weatherfax and RTTY broadcasts.

Having said this, there are many users out there, and for those with the enthusiasm, this can be a very satisfying and low cost way of staying in touch, without being reliant on satellite communications.

Amateur (ham) radio

Where an SSB transceiver works on dedicated marine frequencies, an amateur (ham) radio lets the (suitably qualified) operator 'work' many more frequencies than those allocated to the marine bands.

Many long distance cruisers will fit a ham radio, in addition to an SSB set (or will have their SSB 'wide-banded'), for access to both the ham and the marine bands. This allows them to chat with other ham radio users, though not to link in to the phone network.

There are 'gateways' available on the ham bands that allow you to send and receive e-mail, though these are not always as reliable as the marine services because they are usually run on a voluntary basis by other ham enthusiasts, rather than as a commercial concern. Apart from this, the same comments apply as for SSB radio, so unless you wish to sit your ham licence in order to communicate with other amateur radio enthusiasts, this choice is not recommended for reliable data communications.

Satellite communications

A satellite communications set is actually a radio transceiver, however instead of transmitting radio signals directly over great distances, a satcom system splits the communication path up into segments. The vessel (ship earth station, or SES) communicates with a geostationary or orbiting satellite. The satellite then passes the transmission down to a land earth station (LES), from where it is routed to its destination over the land telephone network.

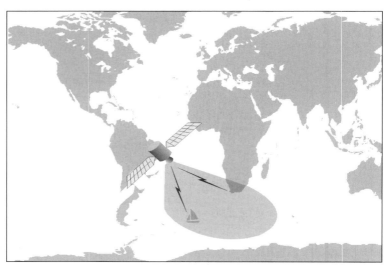

Satellite 'footprint' – both the vessel and 'land earth station' must have a satellite in view to permit simultaneous two-way communications

INMARSAT C   One of the first satellite communications systems available, INMARSAT C offers text-only messaging using a small omni-directional antenna. Your PC is used as a terminal for sending and receiving messages, which can go out as e-mail, fax, or even as SMS (mobile phone text) messages. Also, as part of the GMDSS system, you can send distress messages, and receive SafetyNet messages (similar to Navtex, containing both weather and navigation information). INMARSAT C units may also be polled from ashore. This allows friends and relatives to track your progress across the oceans through websites such as www.purplefinder.com.

Complete INMARSAT C system. Trimble's 'Galaxy' terminal software runs well on a standard PC

INMARSAT C coverage is effectively worldwide, just stopping at latitudes above about 70 degrees North and South.

The equipment is fairly inexpensive, but the message costs are relatively high, so if you are going to be sending and receiving a lot of messages it may be worth looking at other systems. System manufacturers supply their own software to run on your PC, or you can purchase more powerful third party software.

INMARSAT D+

INMARSAT D+ is a very simple device used primarily for polling the position of a vessel from ashore, and also for applications such as remote monitoring and control of equipment. It is used by some organised events such as the ARC for tracking the positions of vessels, but is not really suited for normal communications.

INMARSAT Mini-M (Satphone, Boatphone)

This system has been the most popular means of voice and data communications for many years, though it is now being challenged by Iridium. A gyro-stabilised dish antenna – typically 25 to 50cm diameter – connects to a controller unit which has a phone handset, a phone jack for a fax machine, and a serial port for a PC. For voice calls it works just like a standard phone. Fax and data run at

INMARSAT's Mini-M system offers voice, fax and data transmissions using spot beam technology

2.4kbps, which is adequate for e-mail but too slow to surf the Internet; it is also a quarter the speed of a standard fax connection. It is not part of the GMDSS system, and coverage is not worldwide – quite a lot of the Pacific is not covered, as well as parts of the South Atlantic and the Indian Ocean.

INMARSAT B

This is the big brother of Mini-M, offering the same coverage as INMARSAT C. It has the same facilities as Mini-M, but with the High Speed Data (HSD) option, data rates are 64kb/s, the same as an ISDN land line. The system can also be part of the GMDSS network and so used for distress calls and the like.

INMARSAT 'B' is not really suitable for smaller yachts since a big and heavy gyro-stabilised satellite dish (1.2 metres diameter) is required. The equipment and installation is also relatively expensive, however for those with larger yachts, who plan to do a good deal of communicating, the cost of INMARSAT B with HSD is very good value for money when calculated as pence per Megabyte.

INMARSAT Fleet

A high performance system which offers similar facilities to INMARSAT B but in a smaller package – the Fleet 77 units available at time of writing have a dish diameter of about 77cm, and look to shrink to 55cm. Equipment and call costs are lower than with INMARSAT B and optionally you can use the packet data service, MPDS, where you are charged by volume of data instead of online time. Coverage is worldwide, 70° North to 70° South.

Iridium

Iridium is in many ways similar to Mini-M in performance, but it uses a large number of satellites in a low earth orbit rather than INMARSAT's four geostationary satellites 'parked' over the equator, so coverage is truly global even in high latitudes, and a small fixed external antenna is used.

The system can use a cellphone type handset, or a fixed base unit.

Equipment and call costs are slightly cheaper than with Mini-M, and Iridium to Iridium calls are notably inexpensive. As well as voice, there is a data service with the same 2.4kb/s data rate as Mini-M, though there is currently no fax service.

Thuraya

This is a satellite communications service covering the Mediterranean, the Gulf and North Africa, though there is talk of extending the service with additional satellites. The phone handset is hand held, like an Iridium phone. It also can take a GSM SIM card, allowing the phone to be used for both GSM and satellite communications. Although coverage is restricted compared to Mini-M or Iridium, its advantage for PC users is that the data rate is 9.6kbps instead of the 2.4kbps those systems offer.

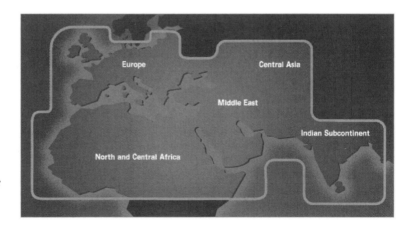

Current coverage of the Thuraya satellite system

Globalstar   Another hand held satellite phone system. Originally promising global coverage, this has shrunk down so it now extends over the Americas, Europe, the Middle East, much of the former Soviet Union, and Australia and New Zealand, plus offshore waters.

Though available in these areas, currently not all operating areas offer data communication facilities.

Orbcomn    This is a simple store and forward text messaging service – there are no voice or fax services. When you enter a message it waits for a satellite to pass overhead and then transmits it; the satellite then sends it to the earth when it next passes over the ground station. Because of the nature of the service, it may take up to quarter of an hour for a message to be sent through the system. Coverage is global, though it is not licenced for use in some countries, particularly in the far east. The Orbcomm unit is fully self contained, with its own display and keyboard.

Satellite TV services

A few years ago some services such as DirecPC in the USA and Europe Online in Europe started providing high speed satellite download services using TV satellites.

These can offer the yachtsman the ability to receive data at amazingly high speeds. The way it works is as follows: you dial in to your Internet Service Provider (using GSM, Mini-M or a land line in the normal way) – all outgoing data from the PC to the Internet goes via this route. However data coming back to the PC is redirected to the service provider's system, where it is encoded for you as a satellite TV signal, combined with other data for other users, and broadcast via the TV satellite. On board, a decoder box receives the broadcast datastream, looking out for data 'addressed' to you. It then extracts your data and decodes it, presenting it to your web browser or e-mail software as normal Internet data. Though a circuitous route, data speeds can be very high – some services providing up to 2000kbps. Since most users receive more data than they send (for example web browsing), this significantly speeds up the service.

In addition to the decoder unit, you will need a satellite TV receiver (as with terrestrial TV, note that there are different standards between Europe and the USA). Also you need to sign up with a service provider which covers your area. Coverage is generally good, but not available offshore where there is no TV satellite coverage.

Forthcoming services

Although many of the start-up satellite communications companies of the last decade have gone spectacularly bankrupt, there are still some new technologies in development. Which ones will come to fruition and which will fall by the wayside is hard to predict though.

Teledesic   This system has had a lot of publicity with its aim of providing a broadband satellite service, covering ocean as well as land areas. Technical details are still vague, but it will probably require a stabilised dish antenna like INMARSAT's Fleet and B services. It will not be a mobile service like the hand held Iridium and Thuraya units. It is scheduled to be available from 2005.

ICO   Another service that for a while looked as though it was going to merge with Teledesic to stave off bankruptcy, but it has now been refinanced and is testing the service at the time of writing. Although ICO states it is targeted at the marine market, details of coverage are not yet clear. It offers voice and data (at up to 144kbps) using a hand-held or fixed unit with an omni-directional antenna.

INMARSAT   INMARSAT is launching its new generation of satellites, which are about a hundred times more powerful than the present generation. This means it should be able to offer high speed data connections with a small antenna, making it suitable for use on many yachts.

Satellite TV systems   Fast developing as two way services for use on land, this may extend to use afloat. Although coverage will not extend into the deep oceans, whether you use it for just receiving or for two way communications it will probably continue to be much cheaper than INMARSAT B or Fleet services, with a higher data rate than either these or the GSM GPRS system.

Tips for using satellite communications

Maritime communications, particularly satellite communications, can be very costly – all calls you make are effectively international and you should bear in mind that cross network and intra-network calls (eg INMARSAT to Iridium, or Mini-M to Mini-M) can be extremely expensive indeed.

Keeping costs down

With the low data rates typically experienced by yachtsmen while at sea, you will need to concentrate on keeping your online time, and therefore call costs to a minimum. There are a few tricks you can employ to improve things:

- When accessing the web, it is well worth switching off background images, sound and animation, as these take a long time to download and are seldom essential. Also keep your favourite web sites listed in your browser's favourites list, so you can go directly there.
- When e-mailing, set your e-mail client software (eg Outlook Express) to send messages in plain text format – this is much more compact than RTF or HTML.
- Set a maximum file download size when at sea – save downloading those large files until you can connect to a land line or use a cybercafé.
- Some e-mail packages, such as Outlook XP, and some ISPs that support the IMAP protocol let you just download the message header and the first few lines of the message. Then, if you don't want the message, you can delete it without downloading it. Also, particularly with a slow link such as Mini-M or Iridium, set the time-outs on the incoming and outgoing mail servers to the maximum.
- When selecting an ISP, a bit of care is needed. Many of the free services require you to dial in from a land line in the country of the ISP, as they make their money by taking a percentage of the call charges. Obviously this will not work on a boat. Also not all ISPs will support data rates down to the 2.4kb/s of Iridium and Mini M. A final point is that it is worth choosing an ISP that has local points of presence (POPs) in the countries you will visit, as these are generally cheaper with a GSM or land line than dialling abroad.

Security

Be sure to install a good anti-virus package and keep it up to date – the number of e-mail viruses has increased astronomically over the past few years. Also consider installing some personal firewall software. Configure your e-mail software so that it will not download links to images or web pages found in incoming e-mails, switch off software that can automatically dial out, for example to download data or check for upgrades.

5 ▪ Weather Information

There are many sources of weather information available to the yachtsman, but access to them is dependent upon the communications equipment on board. Unless indicated otherwise, this information is available free of charge.

Weatherfax

Weatherfax consists of synoptic (current weather) and forecast maps produced by meteorologists, covering information such as pressure, wind, weather, sea state and currents, and even icing. There is extensive coverage of Northern Europe, North America and the Caribbean, with maps transmitted regularly over HF single side band (SSB) radio. As well as being receivable on a dedicated weatherfax receiver, they can be received on an SSB radio interfaced to a PC that is equipped with suitable software.

Although it can take some experience to successfully receive and interpret weatherfax images, this is a very low cost way of adding a high-quality meteorological facility to your on board PC system. With practice, mariners should be able to get a better understanding of current and impending weather than would be possible with

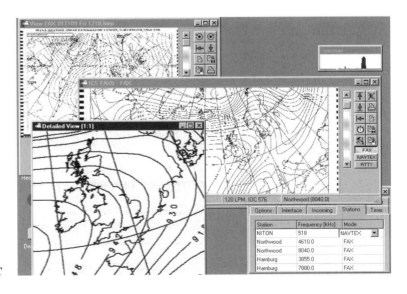

Typical weatherfax images that may be received using an SSB radio connected to a PC

other methods on their own. Particularly when interpreted together with other forecast information (spoken forecasts and shore station reports, NAVTEX etc), weatherfaxes can be very useful indeed.

A simple weatherfax package will typically come supplied with a 'demodulator' that connects the audio output port of the radio to the PC's serial port. With these basic, low cost systems, scheduling and tuning of the radio is left to the user, but they are capable of surprisingly high-quality results.

More sophisticated systems are able to control suitable radios (eg the ICOM PCR-1000 and the Lowe HF-150) and may be set up to automatically tune the radio in to a suitable schedule of frequencies (using a serial connection to the PC's COM port), and use the PC's line-in connector on the sound card to obtain even higher quality images.

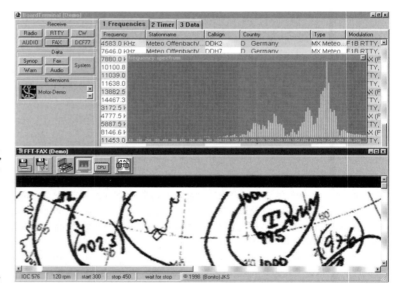

With radio control, scheduling, tuning scopes and image enhancement tools, some systems offer the user powerful control of weatherfax receipt

Weatherfax is a very useful weather resource for yachtsmen and should be available free of charge for the near future. You only need an SSB receiver and suitable antenna to receive weatherfax, not a complete SSB transceiver, so the equipment is not expensive. Do bear in mind that the information you receive using weatherfax is not generally designed for the layman, and to get the most out of received charts you may need to study a suitable guide.

The same data may be available in a number of other ways, for example the UKMO puts some UK weather charts up on its web site which are transmitted as weatherfaxes, as well as offering a faxback service using a premium rate phone number.

From a European perspective, the best weatherfax transmissions are currently from Hamburg (formerly Offenbach) with the UK transmissions from Northwood being nearly as good if not quite as frequent or as reliable. The stations tend to transmit images simultaneously on different frequencies, so it is usually possible to get good pictures in spite of adverse atmospherics.

For new users and for those who have tried and discounted weatherfax because they have been unable to receive suitable quality images, consider the following, which may help.

- Your greatest enemies are poor antenna installation (and grounding) and electrical interference. If you experience interference while listening to programmes on other frequencies, you will have trouble receiving weatherfax. Solution: identify the source of the interference and switch it off! RF (radio frequency) energy behaves differently from DC electricity – even those with good knowledge of the latter may require some help with the former.
- When tuning, remember to tune the radio *down* for USB transmissions and *up* for LSB ones. Judge when it looks right on screen rather than blindly sticking to the nominal 1.9kHz amount.
- Hearing the signal is very important to successful tuning – if your radio switches off its speakers when you plug in the demodulator, try adding a 'Y' connector and a separate speaker. Experienced operators can hear when the signal is 'right'.
- There are many controls on the average radio receiver. Change only one thing at a time and wait for it to settle down. If it makes no difference, change it back before changing anything else or you'll get lost.
- Very few people get it right first time – be prepared to spend some time perfecting your skills. Long winter evenings are ideal, and with a PC you won't be wasting paper and ink.

It can also be challenging identifying which transmissions should be listened out for. Whilst each station usually transmits its own schedule of broadcasts at frequent intervals, for the new user, up-to-date details of transmission schedules are contained within the UK Hydrographic Office's *Admiralty List of Radio Signals, vol 3*. There are also several private publications offering listings, and the Internet is a good source of this type of information.

Synoptic reports (SYNOP)

As part of the data sharing agreements of the WMO (World Meteorological Organisation), current weather (synoptic) reports are transmitted over SSB radio in an encoded text format called SYNOP. The data is sent in groups of five characters, and the traditional way of decoding this was to look up each set of characters in a code book, and transcribe it to text. However, modern weather packages will not only receive the data, but also decode it and display weather reports at each station. Some can even interpolate the data to draw a weather map.

SYNOP data sent consists of current values (as well as trends) for air pressure, wind speed and direction, sea state, air and sea temperature, cloud cover, precipitation and much more, typically updated every 6 or 12 hours.

If you receive SYNOP information regularly, some weather software allows you to create animated sequences from stored data – this can be very useful in anticipating future weather.

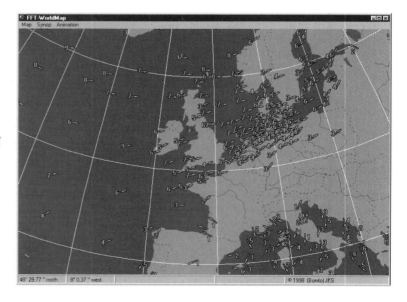

Viewing historical sequences of synoptic (current) data can be nearly as informative as studying professional forecasts in helping to predict the weather

NAVTEX

A navigational information service that carries weather forecast information, particularly severe weather warnings. It is transmitted in English on 518kHz, and in many countries, in a local language, on 490kHz. These transmissions are broadcast every four hours, with a nominal range of 200–300 nautical miles, and can be received with a dedicated NAVTEX receiver. Similar information is transmitted over the INMARSAT C SafetyNet service, though where there is NAVTEX coverage the SafetyNet data is geared towards the offshore mariner. In areas that are not implementing NAVTEX, or where NAVTEX coverage is poor SafetyNet data can be very detailed

As part of the Global Maritime Distress and Safety System (GMDSS), NAVTEX is a free and pretty reliable source of weather information, with steadily improving coverage and information available.

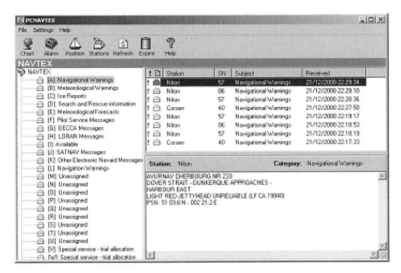

Dedicated NAVTEX software makes it very easy to manage messages

Yachtsmen who already have a PC and an SSB receiver on board may, with the addition of simple software, receive these broadcasts on their PC. Most weatherfax software can receive NAVTEX messages, but for those not interested in weatherfax, dedicated NAVTEX software is available.

The NAVTEX system is really designed for unattended operation using a dedicated receiver unit. Using a PC however gives you a useful and flexible independent NAVTEX system at low cost, running in the background whilst you use your chart plotter.

Weather satellite images

Weatherfax is a great source of current and forecast weather reports, but there are many parts of the world where it is not available, and this is where weather satellite systems come into their own. A weather satellite system is usually supplied as a complete package of antenna, receiver and software. Operation is easier than weatherfax because the software predicts when the satellites are transmitting, automatically tunes in the receiver and receives the transmitted images for you, totally unattended. The receiver can be mounted at deck level, but should be kept clear of sources of electrical and radio interference as the satellite transmission power is very low, only 5W, transmitted from about 600 miles away.

Whilst most of the sources of weather information discussed so far provide weather data that has been prepared by meteorologists, weather satellite images provide raw weather information. This means that there is no time lag in its preparation, so it is always much more up-to-date than other sources. The downside is that you need to do all the analysis yourself, so to get the most from these systems, you should have at least a passing acquaintance with meteorological practices.

All boats can receive polar satellite images, known as Wefax, which are on a North–South circumpolar orbit, with each orbit taking about 100 minutes. In mid latitudes they typically pass overhead three or four times a day, but at higher latitudes the passes become more frequent as the satellites converge towards the poles. The satellite takes a continuous photograph of the patch of earth beneath it, simultaneously transmitting it down to any receivers un-

A small decoder, attached to an antenna is all that is required, in addition to a standard PC

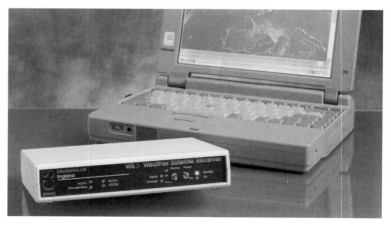

der its path. You receive a rectangular strip aligned approximately N–S, and the higher the satellite rises above your horizon the greater the area covered.

In fact it is actually taking two photographs – one with visible light and the other infra-red (both as grey scale images). The visible light image is great for showing the textures of the top of the cloud, through the shadows cast, and also for picking up patches of sea fog which do not show up on the infra-red images, but they are only available during the day. Infra-red images effectively measure temperature, so they are available at all times. If there is cloud, they

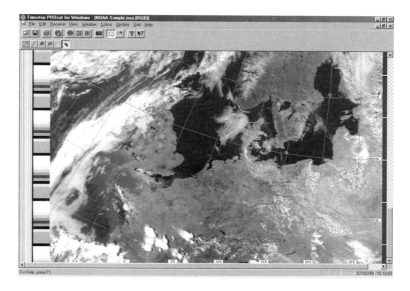

Composite image of NW Europe created from NOAA weather images (visible and infra-red)

pick up the temperature of the top of the cloud – and the colder it is, the higher the cloud top is. When there is no cloud it picks up the sea or land temperature, which can show thermal currents such as the Gulf Stream, and also pick up icing. The weather satellite software can then add coastlines and a grid to these images (very useful when there is extensive cloud cover), and also combine them into a realistically coloured image that combines the information held in each individual image.

Boats large enough to have a stabilised dish antenna installed can also track geostationary satellites 'parked' over the equator – a dish antenna is required because these satellites are at a very high altitude, producing a very weak signal. Because of their altitude, geostationary satellites can see the whole hemisphere (which it divides up into smaller sections), so the area of weather that can be seen is much greater than with orbiting satellites. Images are transmitted at regular intervals of about 30 minutes, which enables very vivid animations to be created. These can be viewed directly on the PC, or transmitted onto the boat's TV system.

Internet weather resources

The weather systems already discussed, including weatherfax, SYNOP, NAVTEX and weathersat are all very useful for the navigator, especially for those going offshore, since they are free to receive, and provide some form of redundancy, being based on different parts of the radio spectrum.

However the Internet has made it possible for the average yachtsman to receive both synoptic and forecast weather information, both conveniently and affordably, while ashore and at sea.

As we will see in Chapter 8 – The Internet, it is not yet feasible for a yachtsman of modest means to be able to 'surf' the Internet whilst more than a few miles offshore. This means that, though a coastal sailor may be able to visit useful websites such as The Meteorologicel Office, the BBC or CNN to obtain weather information, he cannot realistically do so while on a voyage at sea.

Mindful of this limiting factor, software manufacturers have devised innovative ways of getting decent weather information to yachtsmen, *without forcing them to visit a web site.*

Few of these services are free, though charges do seem to be modest when one considers the up-to-dateness and usefulness of the information they provide.

E-mail services

The most basic way of receiving prepared weather information via the Internet is to buy a subscription from a meteorological supplier to receive text forecasts for a fixed or open-ended period. They will usually want to know your cruising area and some basic information about your boat, for example your cruising speed.

That's it – simply dial-up in the normal way (using a cellphone or satellite connection) and a text forecast drops into your inbox.

If the weather forecasts are for a long voyage, say an Atlantic crossing, they'll want to know your route in advance and will probably want you to send them a short daily e-mail with your position and details of the weather you are actually experiencing.

GRIB files

Some electronic charting software is able to read and display the GRIB weather file format. GRIB files are actually packets of weather information that have been compressed. Once downloaded from the Internet and decompressed, suitable software can read and display animated weather forecasts on top of an electronic chart.

There are various sources of this information available. Some suppliers offer a paid subscription service where the GRIB file is sent as an e-mail attachment.

Free GRIB files can often be downloaded too, but this will require you to use your Internet browser to visit a web site in order to get the file and this can be very slow and expensive, especially if connected to the Internet using a satellite service such as Inmarsat C or Mini-M.

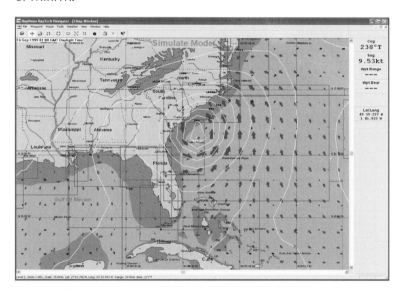

Raymarine's Raytech Navigator showing pressure and ocean currents from a GRIB file

Though GRIB files are a useful and affordable source of weather information, quality can vary. For those requiring consistent quality forecasts, from known and reliable sources, a number of proprietary services have been developed.

Proprietary services

These services really extend the concept of GRIB files, by providing information in a form that is highly compressed in order to minimise expensive satellite or cellular communication time. However they let the yachtsman control just how much information he wants to receive, and for what geographical area.

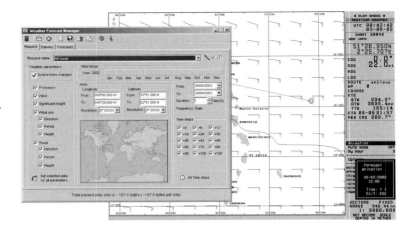

Transas' Weather Wizard, showing host and display software. It can also display this information in their electronic charting system

The yachtsman uses a small piece of 'host' software whilst offline to determine which weather parameters he wants to receive, for example, pressure, wind, sea state etc, and for what period. The complete 'request' is placed in his e-mail outbox, and when he dials up, is transitted as an attachment to the supplier's computer.

Here, the request is processed automatically and a forecast is prepared, compressed and sent back to the yachtsman's e-mail address, usually in about ten minutes.

The yachtsman dials-up again and the 'host' software retrieves the forecast, decompresses it, and prepares it for use with standalone viewing software or within electronic charting software.

This is good information – the above system helped the author cross the Atlantic safely from the Cape Verdes to the Caribbean in eleven days – without an engine!

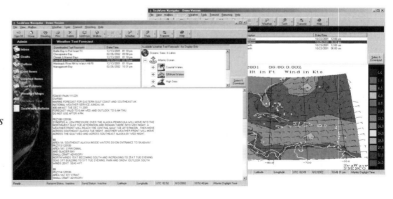

A variety of systems exist, offering both text and graphical forecast information

Vessel administration programs can cover a wide range of facilities, but they all have one thing in common: to make the running of the vessel easier.

The usefulness of these programs is not confined to the complex and sophisticated systems to be found on board superyachts – as smaller pleasure yachts get increasingly complex and include more and more systems, it can be extremely challenging for the skipper of a small boat to keep a handle on all the important aspects of running the boat.

Boat management

A simple system will offer a convenient place to store much of the myriad information that needs to be close to hand when running a boat. This might include information about the boat itself, its ownership and registration, yacht club, marina and insurance details, spares and inventory, crew and supplier details, even basic maintenance schedules and records.

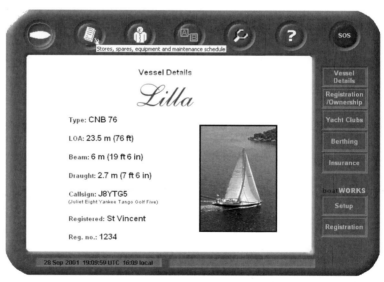

Simple management software helps the owner or skipper by storing useful information in one place

More powerful systems can cope with tracking expenses (and also income for charter boats), act as a store or an index for the boat's documentation, and provide sophisticated functions for monitoring the boat's systems.

Many of the more powerful boat management systems offer very sophisticated functions, but some have a better user interface than others, and some can be configured to suit the user's specific needs whereas with others everything in the program is fixed.

Documentation The most sophisticated systems are nowadays likely to be supplied with your new boat. A modern boat, of even moderate size includes an enormous amount of systems and will probably be subject to European or national legislation requiring a certain level of documentation to be provided.

A package such as *Techman* will let all those involved in the project – designer, boatyard, project manager and owner – track the whole process, beginning with the initial specification, obtaining costings and quotations, through the entire build process. This provides the owner with a complete 'as built' specification. This can be used as the basis for planning future work on the vessel. Though a considerable effort to enter all of the data into the PC, when carried out through the build process (as is necessary to track the project anyway) it should not be too onerous a task.

Large amounts of information associated with the building of a boat may be stored for the owner in an on-board system

Once a boat is handed over to the owner it comes with a huge pile of manuals, drawings and specifications covering everything from light fittings to the generator. On a larger yacht this can easily run to several bookshelves of documentation, and it can be a nightmare to find the right manual. Much of this documentation is already provided on CD-ROM or DVD by some builders.

Systems monitoring

In manual systems, a human enters information into the system. The next stage, extensively used on larger yachts, is to use a PC-based systems monitoring package. Sensors automatically pass information to the PC about different parts of the vessel, where it is displayed, logged and stored, and can be used to alert of impending problems, spot trends or help diagnose faults.

Whilst not as exciting as chart plotting, communications or weather, these systems can make boat management a much easier process, particularly as boats become more complex.

Clear presentation of power system data for a medium size motor yacht

As well as monitoring systems on board, some of the systems available will also send a message ashore via GSM or satellite if an alarm arises, such as a bilge or fire alarm or low battery state, or they will allow the user to connect in to the boat from a PC ashore, either by dialling in directly or via the internet, to monitor and control systems. This is ideal for the owner who wants to be able to check on the status of his boat when he lives some distance away.

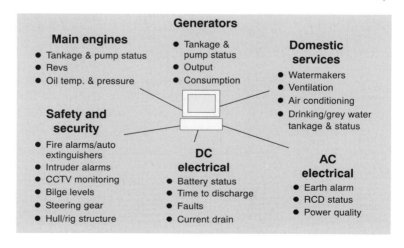

Sophisticated monitoring systems will become commonplace on smaller yachts in the future

Video monitoring

It used to require a specialist interface card for a PC to be able to drive video cameras to monitor the engines, to monitor blind spots or allow the sails to be checked from down below, or as a security system. Now, simple systems can be created at very low cost, by using cameras based on the webcams that are popular in the home and office. Once video imagery is in the computer, it can easily be made available across an on-board network, or even accessed by a shore station so you can check on the boat's security remotely.

There are a number of options with cameras. Colour is obviously available, but mono or infra-red cameras operate much better in low light levels or at night. Also some cameras offer the facility to have a remotely operated pan and tilt or zoom function, which can be controlled from the PC.

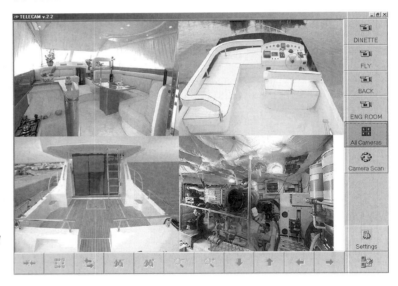

Complex systems can monitor multiple cameras at the same time; the cameras are remotely triggered by heat or motion sensors

This may seem like science fiction, but small video cameras really are surprisingly inexpensive nowadays. With their low power consumption, they are ideally suited to 'keeping an eye' on areas of a vessel that may be hazardous or impracticable to check regularly.

The PC is an ideal system for gathering, displaying and recording all of this information. Smaller yachts can have one or two fixed cameras interfaced to the PC via a USB port or a video capture card. Larger yachts may have multiple cameras with pan, zoom and tilt capabilities working with a video matrix unit that also interfaces to the boat's security system.

7 ▪ Training and Entertainment

Having examined the wealth of marine software now available, we have seen how using a PC on board can help you get more out of your sailing while planning passages and actually under way. It does not stop there, however, because the 'multimedia' capabilities of newer computers are ideally suited to delivering high-quality educational and entertainment material.

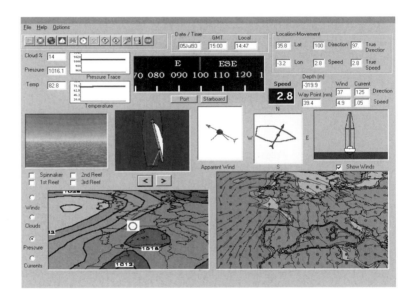

Comprehensive modelling of many variables can make these systems realistic, which aids understanding

Learning can be enjoyable!

As well as excellent programs to help you learn new skills (or at least the theory) during long winter evenings when the boat is laid up, there are also many training programs that can help you brush up your skills during the season.

Taking on board the maxim that 'to be effective, learning must be fun', software manufacturers have written training packages that are not only educational, but enjoyable to use as well. It is not uncommon to see and hear full colour video simulations, along with log books and course material structured so you can learn at your own pace.

And if such 'edutainment' weren't enough, the PC is an ideal platform for playing purely recreational games and, increasingly, for viewing full-length feature films on DVD. This is great for keeping bored children occupied or for those times when the row to the Happy Yottie across a rainy anchorage just doesn't appeal!

Training software may be split broadly into simulators and tutors; whilst some simulators offer self-test facilities, tutors nearly always include some element of simulation as well.

Simulators

Often at sea there are many things going on at once. The sailor may not have the luxury of time to evaluate the cause and effect of his actions in isolation from external factors. Simulator programs are an attempt to do just that, to take one aspect of the navigator's craft and to allow him to practise it in controlled conditions to increase his skills.

Because real world factors are modelled in the program, users are presented with a fairly lifelike representation of what they might experience at sea – without the mêlée of wind, tide, boat, crew, visibility etc which often serve to hinder the learning process.

Thus the user can practise such skills as the recognition of lights, buoyage, sound signals, even Morse code. The idea is that if the simulation is realistic enough, is repeated often enough and is not too predictable, then the skill becomes second nature.

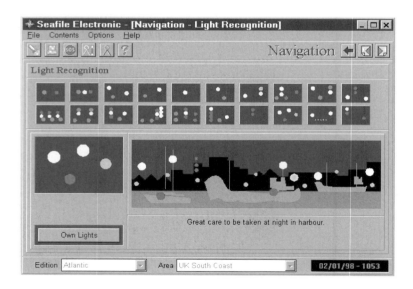

One of the best uses for training software is in navigation light recognition

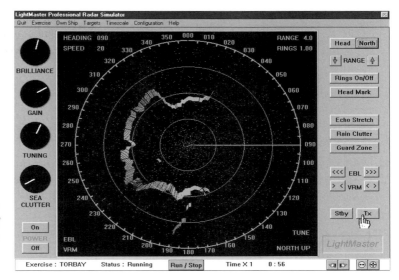

Simulators help yachtsmen master many complicated controls to get the best out of a radar set

Simulators are ideal for more complex learning situations based around modern technology – for the occasional yachtsmen, coping with the range of functions available on modern radars and DSC radios can be challenging. Relying on such equipment without full knowledge of its operational behaviour could well be

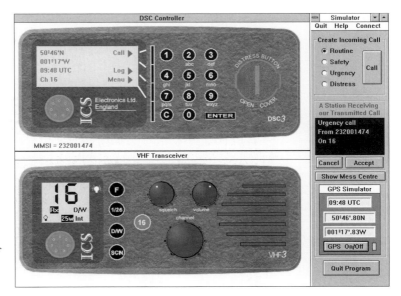

A DSC Simulator enables a yachtsman to practise for distress situations without the risk of sending a false GMDSS alert

dangerous – bad decisions can be made due to misinterpretation of information that the equipment supplies.

Radar simulators teach you how the various controls affect the clarity of the received image. Again, the simulator models various environmental conditions (rain, waves etc) and their effect on the image may be seen, such feedback aiding the learning process.

The introduction of the GMDSS means that more and more yachtsmen are fitting VHF Digital Selective Calling (DSC) radios on board. Whilst DSC automates many traditionally spoken radio tasks, such as calling up other vessels or initiating distress calls, the change in method has been challenging for many. A DSC simulator lets you practise using a typical set, without the worry of initiating a false distress alert on a 'live' DSC radio. Simulators generally have fairly low computer requirements and do not require connections to external equipment.

Tutors

Where simulators excel is in aiding recognition; however, they are seldom suitable as aids to actual understanding of topics. This is where tutors come in. Tutors tend to take full advantage of the PC's multimedia capabilities, offering structured learning courses for the beginner right through to the experienced mariner. Tutor programs are available which cover navigation, seamanship, meteorology, even the collision regulations.

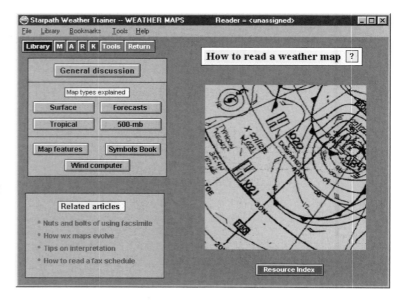

Tutors come in all shapes and sizes and, if well designed, can really help in understanding a new topic

Most programs are organised into a series of instructional 'chapters', each covering a particular topic and linked together with reference material. Often they will have extensive glossaries, with pictures, and even sound and video footage, to aid your understanding. Many programs boast a log book, where you can record your progress through the system, as well as question and answer sections to measure your understanding of the material.

As with printed educational material, the usefulness of a particular program to any individual student varies enormously and is a very personal thing. For this reason, you should take the opportunity of trying out this kind of software before purchase, if at all possible.

Many yachting magazines review computer training packages in their book pages and may be able to advise you; but better still, avoid the classified advertisements and visit a marine computing specialist where you may be able to try before you buy.

Games

The worldwide computer games industry is massive and growing very quickly – high-quality interactive multimedia presentation of action, arcade and more intellectual gameplay is a compelling combination, whether played to help unwind after a busy day at work, or simply as an alternative to more passive televisual entertainment.

On board, the same is true and computer games can certainly help while away long hours on passage. But games are quite demanding upon a PC, with heavy use of graphics. If you rely on your PC

With sound and video capability, educational programs can be surprisingly realistic

for critical navigation tasks, bear in mind that some of the 'big name' resource hungry games can cause problems with the machine's configuration, causing other programs to stop working properly.

If you insist on using such games software on your boat's PC, install it and thoroughly check that it has not had an adverse effect on your other programs well before you go to sea – although it's unlikely that such a game will actually damage your PC permanently, it may be necessary to reinstall and reconfigure all your 'proper' software from scratch if you experience a problem.

That said, most games are pretty well behaved, particularly ones aimed at the yachting market. Similar to educational simulator programs, the current crop of games have far more options and better graphics than their 'serious' cousins. There are games available that let you take the helm of cruising and racing yachts and powerboats, with realistic scenery, even computer controlled 'virtual opponents' to compete against.

TV and video playback

As the price of high resolution flat screen TFT panels has and continues to plummet, they have become increasingly attractive as replacements for CRT-based TV sets. They also offer relatively low power consumption, small size and ease of panel mounting.

If you want to watch television, you can add a TV tuner as an expansion card in your desktop PC, or add a tuner box between the PC and the display. Some laptops already include a TV tuner facility. With most of the tuner cards and boxes, you can attach a terrestial TV antenna, or even a satellite decoder. **Tip:** to get the best audio playback from your PC, feed the output from the sound card into the Aux input of the boat's stereo system.

Also, the Digital Versatile Disc (DVD) has now come of age – for the first time, it is possible to have a full-length, full-motion feature film stored on one CD-ROM sized disc. The DVD is already replacing video cassettes as a distribution medium and, being digital, is ideally suited to work with your on-board PC. In fact DVD is increasingly fitted as standard to desktop and laptop PCs.

Given that very few yachtsmen actually record TV programmes on board, it looks likely that DVD will completely replace video cassettes for playback. Especially when you consider that the DVD is physically much smaller than a video cassette as well as being much more reliable in the marine environment.

See also page 125 for information on television and DVDs.

8 ▪ The Internet

The last few years have seen an explosion in the growth of the Internet and few would deny that this growth will accelerate even faster in the coming years. The Internet, or at least parts of it, are increasingly becoming available through digital television services.

So what is this phenomenon, and could it be useful to yachtsmen?

An Internet history primer

In its early years, the Internet was a little bit like the old American Wild West, a 'place' inhabited by computer scientists, enthusiasts and hackers, who delighted in its informality and complexity and in getting around the limitations of the early technology.

For the Internet to grow, this had to change, and change it has; its various parts now dovetail so neatly with current communications/ marketing/entertainment media that it has become a compelling technology that is hard to avoid – even if we should want to. Nowadays, the Internet offers worldwide users a simple, low cost and convenient method of communicating (written, audio and visual), learning and trading, even of delivering certain types of products (software and data).

There must be very few yachtsmen who are not aware of the Internet or who have not used the World Wide Web

Internet basics

The Internet is an informal global network of computers, which are connected together by ordinary telecommunications cables. What makes it special is that the computers all speak the same digital language (or protocol) – TCP/IP – and so can communicate conveniently. The Internet's computers are connected like a spider's web so that there are many different possible pathways from one router to another. TCP/IP takes transmitted data and breaks it down into conveniently sized 'packets' that are then transmitted across the Internet's pathways and reassembled at the other end. Should a packet become damaged in transit (corrupted) or not arrive for any other reason, it will be sent again, often by a different pathway, until all is received and reassembled correctly.

So if a computer should break down, or if a communications link be broken or overloaded with traffic, the 'fault-tolerant' Internet will adapt to make sure that robust communications are nearly always available.

The end-user (that's you) doesn't usually see this behind-the-scenes work – typically, the Internet user is using the Internet through an organisation called an Internet service provider (ISP) whose computers are linked directly to the Internet. Once you've connected to your ISP (often through a phone line), they look after the business of sending and receiving your 'traffic' onto the Internet proper.

It's important to note that the Internet is not owned by anyone. There is not a global organisation that has somehow put the infrastructure in place for the Internet to be. However, it is obviously very costly for such an infrastructure to exist, so who pays for all the computer hardware, cabling and software engineering required?

Ultimately of course, the user pays. This is usually done in one of two ways. Firstly, the end-user pays their ISP a small annual or monthly fee and the ISP pays a much larger fee to the telecommunications company that actually provides the communications service. The second and increasingly common way is for the ISP to provide access free of direct charge to the user; but the ISP gets paid a percentage of each user's telephone charges by the phone company.

Even the telecommunications giants are not large enough to build complete worldwide networks themselves, so they tend to come to arrangements between themselves, whereby they agree to carry each other's traffic on a sort of swap basis. This is very similar to how the original postal and telephone systems developed, and because the telecommunications companies are all using equipment which speaks the same protocol (TCP/IP), the Internet has been able to grow very quickly into a large, powerful and reliable system.

This is all very well for onshore users, using powerful PCs and land-line connections direct to the Internet, but sadly not all of the benefits of the Internet are currently available to today's yachtsmen.

There are, though, some aspects that are incredibly useful for yachtsmen, and taking the time to have a grasp of basic concepts that are often 'hidden' from our shore-bound cousins allows you to get much more from the Internet than you might think.

Internet for yachtsmen

The Internet actually comprises an enormous range of tools and facilities, with strange names like FTP, WWW, Gopher, Telnet, POP3, IRC, WAIS, Finger, Ping etc. Usually, when you have access to the Internet through an ISP, you can use most or all of these tools if you should want to. Do not be alarmed, though – the useful ones are normally set up for you automatically, and most yachtsmen only ever use the three or four really important tools – **e-mail**, the **World Wide Web, FTP** and sometimes **newsgroups**.

As a yachtsman, which of these you use, and how often, will depend upon two factors: what kind of sailing you do, and what kind of Internet access you have.

E-mail

Electronic mail is a fantastically useful tool – allowing you to send and receive messages worldwide, at incredibly low cost; it can contain pictures, sounds, even videos. Even better, e-mail is an asynchronous (or store and forward) system – unlike the telephone, where both parties have to be present to conduct a conversation, once you have sent an e-mail, it waits on the recipient's 'mail server' (a kind of electronic post office) until they log in and collect it. If for any reason the e-mail doesn't arrive (maybe you misspelled the address?), the Internet will 'bounce' the e-mail back to you, so you know your message didn't get through.

Virtually all Internet users ashore have access to and use e-mail. On board, e-mail is often the only part of the Internet that yachtsmen currently use, because simple text messages do not require a fast connection. Assuming you have the relevant account set up and suitable equipment on board, it is quite possible to send and receive e-mail via a 'slow' connection such as a GSM mobile phone, INMARSAT C or Mini-M unit or even MF/HF SSB radio.

With some modern satellite systems, you don't even need to have a PC on board to send and receive e-mail messages. However,

The Internet offers seamless connectivity between computers all over the world

even with these systems, using a PC with an available serial port makes life much simpler because you can use the PC's keyboard and access the system's functions much more easily.

For more information on communications including e-mail, see chapter 4.

The World Wide Web

Also known as the WWW or simply 'the web', the World Wide Web lets Internet users access or 'browse' web sites of prepared information. Virtually all marine equipment manufacturers now maintain web sites, containing product and price information as well as links to other web sites containing related information.

This can be an invaluable resource for marine users. Imagine the scenario when, for example, in an unfamiliar harbour with a failed water pump for your engine: connect to the Internet and access the engine manufacturer's web site, then browse their parts list and distributor list to ascertain the part you require and your nearest agent. You have a query? E-mail the technical department for further information. No local dealer? Order direct, pay by credit card and have the part shipped by courier.

WWW access requires a more powerful connection to the Internet than does e-mail, so access to the WWW when sailing offshore is currently restricted to superyachts and commercial vessels. Leisure yachtsmen *can* browse the WWW reasonably well from their PC, using a GSM cellphone, but if you do this, set your web browser to display just text, with all images and sound switched off, as this will significantly improve performance. Also, some well appointed marinas are offering a shore phone line, which eliminates any communications problems when you are tied up alongside.

This situation will improve over the next few years and it seems certain that very soon it will be possible (and affordable) for ordinary yachtsmen to enjoy the same kind of access speeds within cellphone range that they enjoy when ashore.

Beyond cellphone range, fast web browsing is unlikely to be within the pocket of the average yachtsman for some time to come.

FTP

File transfer protocol, or FTP, is a means of downloading information from the Internet to your PC. This may often be data, such as weather information, or programs, such as a demo version of an application or the latest software release. Access to FTP sites is generally made through your web browser, but if you use a separate FTP program you'll find that files generally download faster, as there is not all of the graphical interface of the web to be downloaded first. FTP also has the facilities allowing you to upload files, rename them, delete them and so on, subject to having the necessary access rights.

You will also find that there are still a few places on the Internet offering a service called remote FTP. This goes back to the early days of the Internet, when a fast modem was 2400 bps, and just about everything was text based. You send a specially formatted e-mail to a remote FTP server with details of the FTP site you want to access, and the files you want to retrieve from it. The server then automatically retrieves the file and sends it to you as an e-mail. This is still the only way to retrieve files if you have a store and forward system, such as INMARSAT C, and it is also generally more efficient than using the web or standard FTP.

Newsgroups

Most Internet users with ordinary dial-up access through an ISP automatically have access to newsgroups – even if they don't know it! Newsgroups are really giant noticeboards to which you can send messages which can then be read by anyone else who visits the newsgroup. In this way, 'threads' or topics of discussion are built up that you may simply read for interest or make your contribution to, if you have something constructive to offer the discussion.

There are an enormous number of newsgroups available to all Internet users – you can be more or less certain there will be groups that address your interests, marine or otherwise. Once you have found one that looks of interest, you 'subscribe' to it – this means that when you dial up, your news software automatically checks the newsgroup for messages that you have not seen yet, and downloads them onto your PC.

As you may imagine, some newsgroups are very active and some are less so; also the quality of discussion (as in real life) can vary enormously. Some newsgroups are unashamedly partisan to one cause or another and others may have overwhelmingly regional, particularly US, bias. However, many newsgroups are 'moderated' by a responsible individual to ensure discussions do not get out of hand or wander from the main thread.

Some very active newsgroups can generate a lot of traffic and for this reason, if you are using newsgroups on board, it is recommended that you subscribe to only those that are of very great interest – newsgroup browsing can be very addictive!

Internet connections from ashore

If you have a PC on board, but do not have a suitable communications system to access the Internet whilst at sea, you can still use your on-board PC to prepare e-mail or fax messages for sending on once you reach your destination.

Usually, access to the Internet is achieved through a local-rate call to your ISP's Point of Presence (POP). Although it is possible to reach your normal POP through the international telephone exchanges, this could work out very costly – and you may need an extremely large number of coins if you are unable to use a credit card or calling card to make the call from a payphone. It makes sense therefore if you are planning to travel widely that you select an ISP which is able to offer local-rate call POPs in most, if not all, your intended destination countries.

Global ISPs and remote e-mail services

One way of getting round this problem is to use a remote e-mail service that you can use via the WWW. Then, all you have to do is to find somewhere you can get access to the WWW (probably using someone else's local-call rate access to their ISP) and to log in to your e-mail account. There are several of these services available, Microsoft's *Hotmail* (http://www.hotmail.com) was one of the earliest and is certainly the most popular with blue-water yachtsmen. Basic access to *Hotmail* remains free of charge, though of course you will probably need to pay someone to get access to the WWW in order to access your account.

Another alternative is to use an ISP that has an international presence. A number of ISPs in different countries have banded together to be able to offer global roaming, which means that in most countries you do not have to make an international call (though there may be a slight surcharge levied to cover the extra costs involved in providing the service).

Alternatively some of the bigger providers such as AOL and CompuServe have local points of presence in most countries, but often their highly graphical user interfaces mean that the link can be unreliable on a slow speed connection.

Hotel telephones

A laptop PC will let you take your data to the phone if you have a built-in modem (which very many do have). This is achieved by simply plugging the modem into a hotel room telephone socket, connecting to the international telephone network, and thence to the Internet.

Bear in mind, though, that there are many different socket types in use worldwide, and that if venturing far it would be wise to invest in one of the adapter sets which are seen at airports and telephone shops. Hotels, of course, have probably the most expensive phones it is possible to use, but in some areas hotels have better maintained lines than may be available otherwise.

Cybercafés

These are popular in many far-flung parts of the world. The basic concept is that you pay a fee per hour or half-hour to access the WWW whilst enjoying a cup of coffee. Typically, a yachtsman would use his on board PC to prepare e-mail messages and would then save them on to a floppy disk that he takes to the local Internet café. Once there, he connects via the WWW to a remote e-mail system, such as *Hotmail, AOL* or *Bigfoot,* so he can send his messages. Whilst on-line, he can also receive any messages that have arrived since he last connected and save them onto disk to be read at leisure on the on-board PC.

One might assume that this facility was confined to more developed parts of the world, but such is the penetration of the Internet that they can be found in cafés and bars, chandleries and harbour offices in the most unlikely and remote places.

Acoustic couplers

There are surprisingly few locations in the world where it is not possible to find a telephone – this is usually the first element of a modern infrastructure that reaches a place, often before mains electricity and sewage. Certainly in more developed parts of the world, it is unusual to be in a dock or harbour without a public telephone being within easy walking distance.

Once the *only* way to connect a computer modem to a phone line, acoustic couplers are nowadays far less common than they used to be, but having one on board could allow you to send e-mails from the most basic public payphone rather than using an expensive hotel phone.

A modem takes digital computer information and turns it into sounds that may be sent down a telephone wire. An acoustic coupler consists of two 'cups' that fit over the telephone mouthpiece and earpiece – it simply transfers the sounds between the telephone and the modem itself. Although inelegant and a little awkward to use, acoustic couplers can often be used where no other method would work.

9 ▪ Choosing a PC System

Currently, it is unusual for marine software products to be sold with a PC included, or indeed for a PC to be sold 'bundled' with marine software. Some specialists do offer this service, which gives you the benefit of a complete, ready to go PC, and this is particularly useful if you want a system of any complexity or if you are new to computers.

Alternatively, if you shop around and buy the components separately you may get a better price (especially if you want a laptop-based solution), though you have the responsibility of making sure that all components of the system meet your needs and are compatible with each other.

In many cases, dealing with an experienced marine computing company will pay dividends in the long run and may cost you less than 'going direct'. This route often gives you better choice, more independent advice and good after-sales service.

First choice: hardware or software?

Deciding on which hardware and software to purchase may appear to be a confusing business, but essentially the process may be approached in one of two ways, and this depends upon whether you already own a PC or not:

If you already have a PC – Find out its specifications and then look for software that will run on it. If you do not already know them, you find out the PC's specifications from the manual you got when you bought it; or right-clicking on the 'My Computer' icon on your desktop will give useful information. Once you have done this, contact a dealer and ask for brochures or catalogues of the types of application you are interested in, and select from packages whose hardware requirements match those of the PC.

If you have not yet bought a PC – If you know which software you want to use, find out the software requirements as described above and then use this as a check-list against the PC specifications when deciding which PC to purchase. Bear in mind that you should always buy a PC that is a little more powerful than you need right now, or that can be upgraded in the future, in case new software comes along that has greater system requirements.

Either way, the key to this process is knowing the specifications of the PC, and the system requirements of the software that you want to run. **The most important thing is that the PC must be powerful enough to run the software. If the software has requirements that exceed the specifications of the PC, it will not run correctly, if at all, so this is a very important stage in making a decision.**

Tip – Sometimes people who do not yet have a PC or software are tempted to buy a PC before choosing the software. This is really the wrong way round because you may end up having purchased a PC which is not powerful enough to do what you want it to, or you may have spent more than you had to on a PC that is far more powerful than you need.

You may have got the impression that you will need the latest and most powerful PC on board. This could not be further from the truth – typically, marine software is not as resource-hungry as other types (for example the latest games, multimedia or large office applications). So while software will always run faster on more powerful PCs, many yachtsmen experience perfectly acceptable performance when using an older, or even second-hand, PC on board.

Computer architecture

Before looking at the individual elements of a computer system, let us first look at the overall architecture of the system.

The 'bus' – linking it all together

Central to the PC is the bus, a kind of nervous system that lets all of the different components of the system talk to each other. In practice, there are a number of different buses in most computers, each with different functions and usually etched onto the 'motherboard'.

The way the different buses and boards are connected together in a PC varies very much according to the PC type – office PC, marine or industrial PC, and laptop.

The 'ISA' bus was the original PC bus, and is now very rarely used except for some sound cards, serial cards and other cards that do not require high performance. Though it will probably survive for quite a while longer, it will become less common because it is much more tricky to set up an ISA device in a PC than a device on a PCI card (see below).

The PCI bus has emerged as the standard high performance bus for the PC. It is significantly faster than the ISA bus partly because

A typical PC motherboard, which carries the 'bus', linking together the system components

the data physically moves around much faster, and also because it was designed to allow cards to move data around more efficiently. Most new cards that are introduced these days are based on the PCI bus, which allows Windows to automate much of the setting-up.

Whilst the ISA and PCI buses can take almost any type of expansion card, the AGP bus was devised exclusively for high performance graphics cards, allowing them to talk directly to the CPU. This allows the same graphics processor to run some 30% faster in the AGP version than in the PCI bus version.

Disk drives are generally interfaced by the IDE bus, whereby each IDE interface can have one or two disks attached, and many PCs have two IDE interfaces. The IDE interface has developed over the years, and now supports CD and CD-RW drives, DVD drives and even backup tapes. The latest Ultra ATA/100 specification is more than fast enough to cope with the fastest disks available today.

The SCSI interface has been widely used for high performance disk drives. Whilst IDE is fine for a single disk, because it has no built-in intelligence the performance starts to drop when there are several IDE devices in the computer. Here the greater built-in intelligence of the SCSI bus offers enhanced performance, so it is most frequently used on servers for multiple hard disks and high performance tape back-ups. Other devices, such as scanners, that would have used the SCSI bus in the past now use the USB bus.

The USB bus has become the standard for external plug-in devices such as cameras, CD drives, scanners, and increasingly printers.

Supported by Windows' 'Plug and Play' technology, you can just plug devices into the PC, and Windows will sort them out for you. A USB hub can be used to give virtually unlimited extra ports – however some devices such as CD writers do not work well through a hub, and are best plugged directly into the computer.

USB runs at 1.2Mb/s, with the new USB2 specification giving 12Mb/s. USB can be used to gain additional serial ports, although we have found that some programs and devices do not work reliably like this – some software won't 'see' the serial port, or it will not cope with the slight differences in timing and behaviour that occur.

Faster than USB is IEEE1394 (also known as Firewire). This is used for things like downloading digital video from a video camera. Fitted as standard on Apple Macs, it is not widespread on PCs.

Another technology just coming into the marketplace is Bluetooth. It is a short range radio interface for connecting peripherals such as printers, phones or cameras to the PC. This looks set to become very popular over the next couple of years.

Components of a PC system

The processor   At the core of the PC system is the CPU (central processing unit) or processor, which controls the system and performs all of the calculations necessary for programs to run.

In the PC market the main manufacturer has been Intel, who have produced PC processors from the very earliest days of the PC. The early 8086 series of Intel processors are of historical interest, and the Pentium range is now offered. Early series of Pentiums (the I, II and MMX) have been phased out, and at the time of writing the Pentium III and IV, and the lower powered Celeron, are current.

Processor speed is measured in MHz or GHz (1 GHz = 1024 x 1MHz) and is important – the higher the speed, the faster the PC runs. In the past it paid to get the fastest processor possible, processor speeds have advanced so much that this is no longer necessary – if you are buying a new computer you will probably find that all the marine software you want will run perfectly adequately on an entry level machine.

Intel does not have a monopoly on processors though; AMD offers a good range of robust processors and these are becoming increasingly popular, particularly for entry level and mid-range systems.

The 'heart' of the PC, the CPU or processor; in this case, a AMD Athlon 1.2GHz model

Also some specialist manufacturers such as Transmeta offer low power processors that could prove popular in PCs for sailing boats, offering a considerable saving in battery drain.

Note that different manufacturers measure the speed of their processors differently, so a 1.2GHz AMD processor does not run at the same speed as a 1.2GHz Pentium 4 processor, for example. Also, as you will see later in this chapter, processor speed is not the only factor in the overall performance of your PC.

It is worth bearing in mind that the speed of computer processors doubles about every 18 months, which is why computers become obsolete fairly quickly.

Very few laptops can have the processor upgraded, however for most desktop type PCs it can be very easy to upgrade the processor by simply plugging a new one into a socket on the motherboard.

Many marine PCs use 'passive backplane' technology, which means that the processor is also easily upgradeable. For some upgrades this simply involves replacing the processor, or if upgrading to a new series of processor, the card that the processor is fitted on may need replacing as well.

Memory (RAM)

When a program is running, as much of the program and its data as possible is copied from the PC's hard disk into Random Access Memory (RAM). This is because it is over a hundred times quicker to read data into the processor from RAM than it is from a hard disk, and a thousand times quicker than from a CD-ROM drive. However, if the program is large, or you are running several programs at once, your PC may not have enough RAM. In this case, the PC will start 'paging' to free up more memory.

This consists of discarding from RAM bits of the program or data that are not currently in use, to make room for those bits that are needed next. Then, when the discarded bits are required again, they are read back in from the hard disk into RAM. Although this is a wasteful process, it allows large programs to run in small amounts of RAM.

RAM chips, packaged as SIMMs, SODIMMS or DIMMs, store data while the PC is switched on

The obvious thing to do is to fit as much RAM as possible into your PC – 128 megabytes (Mb) is the absolute minimum that should be fitted, but 256 or 512Mb has become the norm. This will keep your entire program in memory, and adding more memory can be a far more cost effective way of increasing your PC's performance than fitting a faster processor. The memory generally comes on small cards holding a number of chips on them, which slot in to sockets in the PC. There are a number of different formats and specifications for memory, so it is worth checking with your computer supplier when upgrading (see chapter 12 Upgrading your PC).

Storage – disks and discs

A computer's RAM memory has two major disadvantages – when the computer is switched off the memory is cleared; and it is difficult to distribute programs or data on memory. For these reasons, a number of disk formats are used for longer term storage.

Hard disk

The hard disk (or drive) is used for permanent storage of programs and data on the PC as well as 'paging' as described. Disk capacity typically extends from 10Gb to 100Gb, and machines other than laptops can generally have up to 4 hard disks installed in them, or many more SCSI disks.

When you first get a new machine, it will probably have much more disk space than its predecessor, and you'll think you will never fill it up. However, as operating systems and programs get larger, you will almost inevitably find that sooner or later it will be almost full, and this will cause problems with larger programs and when printing. It is generally much easier to add another disk to a machine than to replace an existing disk with a larger one since most desktop and marine PCs can support several hard disks at once.

Disks and discs (the former use a magnetic technology to store information, the latter, optical) can be conveniently divided into two categories: read-only media and rewritable media.

Read only media

CD-ROM and DVD discs

For some years, PCs have been fitted with drives able to read the 'Compact Disc Read Only Memory' or CD-ROM disc. These drives were usually also able to read commercially produced music CDs. As programs and data sizes got larger, the CD-ROM became a more reliable and lower cost medium than the floppy disk for distributing software. Some programs, in particular games, will often run directly from the CD-ROM, but most office and marine programs are installed from the CD-ROM to the hard disk. This is just as well, as CD-ROM drives are all significantly slower than hard disks, and also are not very reliable when the boat is bouncing around at sea.

A CD-ROM has a maximum storage capacity of 640Mb, but can come in a number of different types or 'formats'. The most common is the CD-ROM, which are pressed from a glass master in large quantities.

The latest variation on this theme is the Digital Versatile Disc (DVD), which is the same physical size as the CD-ROM, but because of a double-sided and/or double layered manufacturing technology, can store several gigabytes of information.

Although identical, DVDs can store many times more data than a CD-ROM

This makes it a suitable format for distributing films, often with a choice of soundtracks and subtitling languages, but this format is also likely to replace the CD-ROM as a means of distributing software in time. DVD drives read both CDs and DVDs.

Rewritable media

The floppy disk

The Double Sided High Density (DSHD) 3.5" floppy disk, with a 1.44Mb capacity used to be the standard method of transferring data between machines; more recently, as data files got much too large to use this medium, and rewritable CDs became common, floppy disk drives have become less so. Indeed, many laptops are now shipped without a floppy disk drive. Nevertheless, they can be very useful (for example preparing e-mails to be sent from an Internet café), so if you have a choice, it is better to have one than not.

Larger/optical rewritable discs

Again, because typical file sizes are so much greater than they were, a variety of higher capacity disc formats have emerged, one of the more popular being Iomega's Zip drive (holding around 100Mb). The large format 'floppy disk' is an appealing concept, but because there are many different incompatible formats, and only a minority of PCs have the necessary hardware fitted as standard, these are not very useful for transferring data between computers.

CD-R, CD-RW and DVD-RAM

With a suitable drive, users can also create their own audio or data CDs, which can then be read by all but the oldest of CD-ROM drives. The main format is CD-R (also known as 'gold' CDs due to their original colour, though this is often silver or metallic blue or green now). With this the CD can only be written to once, which is ideal for long term archival storage of programs or data.

Currently, CD-R media is available in 640/650Mb and 700Mb sizes and may be rated according to how quickly it may be written to (8 x speed, 10 x speed etc). 700Mb CD-Rs, especially those written-to at high speed, may not always be readable on all CD-ROM drives, so if it is important that the CD-R you 'burn' can be read by all, stick to 640Mb discs.

Another useful format is CD-RW, which is a rewriteable format, which can also be used for back-up purposes. With CD-RW discs, when a file is deleted using Microsoft Windows it is not actually deleted from the CD-RW until it is wiped clean, by 'reformatting' or 'initialising', so with time the disc can fill up with deleted files.

DVD-RAM (for Random Access Memory) as opposed to DVD-ROM (for Read Only Memory) is the next generation of storage media. Currently very expensive, it is likely that these drives will become very common over the life of this book.

The display

Almost all displays used on leisure boats are flat panel displays – they will either be built into a laptop PC or supplied as separate displays – for example, for bulkhead mounting.

Flat panels are now very affordable, and have also become available in larger sizes. Compared with traditional cathode ray tube (CRT) displays, these displays offer greater reliability, more compact size and lower power consumption which makes them ideal for the job of on board computing.

Choosing a display

When choosing a flat panel display, consider the following factors:

- **Physical size**, measured diagonally from corner to corner. Most laptops offer anything between a 12.1″ and 13.5″to 14″ display – 12.1″ is the smallest practical size for electronic charting. At the other end of the scale, TFT displays up to 22″, or even up to 60″ (using 'plasma' technology), are available.
- **The resolution**, measured in pixels (dots) across and down the display. This is generally tied in with the screen size, so 12.1″ displays are generally 800x600 resolution (also known as SVGA), with 13.5″ to 14″ displays offering 1024x768 or higher (XGA) resolutions.
- **The number of colours**. Early flat screens could only display 256 colours simultaneously, which was quite limiting on graphics programs. Now, a display should offer at least 17 million colours, depending upon the amount of graphics memory fitted to the PC's display adapter (often 4, 8 or 16Mb).
- **The technology**. Most common is the TFT display, which is what we would recommend for normal use. Less expensive, and now almost obsolete, is the STN (or dual scan) display; these are not recommended because they have relatively poor viewing angles and refresh rates. Finally, there is the transflective or reflective display, which is ideal for use on deck as it excels in bright light conditions, using a mirror behind the display to illuminate it rather than a backlight. At present this is new technology, and the viewing angles and colour range are not as good as with standard TFT displays.
- **The brightness**. For marine use, a display must be bright enough to be seen in bright light and capable of being dimmed right down in darkness to maintain the userís night vision. The brightness of a display is measured in candela/m2 (also known as NITS in the USA). Most office grade and laptop displays are rated at around 150–300 candela/m2, which is fine for use in areas sheltered from direct sunlight. For use on deck or in a wheelhouse it is worth paying the extra to get a high brightness 1500 candela/m2 display or a transflective one, so that you can read it in all lighting conditions.

Often on a bigger boat you may want a number of repeater displays. The easiest way is to use a graphics card with multiple outputs or an external video splitter. Going on from here, combined keyboard, video and mouse switching units allow almost any combination of screens and PCs.

Use good quality video cabling – if the cabling is not of suitable quality for the length, you will see a reduction in image quality, most frequently in a ghosting of the image. Be careful when mixing screen resolutions. You may have problems if, for example, you have a 15" 1024x768 display at the chart table, but only have space for a 12" 800x600 display at the helm position.

Keyboard

Many marine programs are designed so the primary input mechanism is the mouse, rather than the keyboard. However, most programs need keyboard input at some stage, so it is essential to have a keyboard available, even if most of the time it is tucked away.

Even if you are using a laptop, which of course includes a built-in keyboard, it is still often sensible to add an external keyboard. Basic keyboards are so cheap (typically under £15.00) that they can be regarded as sacrificial and are a very good way of keeping the laptop dry. As well as normal office-type keyboards, very compact, water resistant and fully waterproof keyboards can be purchased from marine computing specialists.

A wide variety of compact and/or waterproof keyboards may be chosen for your PC

The two pictures show 5-pin DIN (left) and PS/2 (right) keyboard connectors

There are two types of connector commonly used for keyboards, the older AT type uses a 5-pin DIN connector (shown in the picture above left), while more modern keyboards use the smaller and more reliable PS/2 connector. Laptop PCs are almost universally fitted with a PS/2 connector, whilst office-type PCs may have a mixture. Adapters are freely available from computer stores to convert between the two kinds of connector.

Many laptops include only one PS/2 connector, which can be used for an external keyboard or a mouse. Usually it is possible to purchase a 'Y' connector, which allows both a keyboard and a mouse to share the same connector on the laptop (check your PC manual to confirm this will work with your computer).

A wireless keyboard is often very useful, as it can be stowed away without having to unplug anything. Radio-based wireless keyboards are preferred to infra-red ones, as the radio signals can pass through non-metallic objects, whereas infra-red beams are easily blocked by objects, or can be unreliable in very bright light.

Pointing devices

Some method of pointing at objects on the PC screen is essential with most marine programs. On board, this is usually accomplished using a mouse or a trackball, though other methods, such as touch-screens and light pens, may be used.

Trackballs are usually preferred to mice, because they can be secured so as not to slide around the navigation area. Some (slightly more expensive) trackballs work by monitoring an optical pattern on the ball itself, rather than by the ball turning small wheels within the mouse. Optical trackballs are better than the traditional type because they work more reliably with damp fingers.

Though more expensive than mice, track balls are to be preferred on board because they stay in one place

On some old PCs and laptops, the mouse was connected using a 9-pin serial port, rather than a dedicated PS/2 connector. Although this is very unusual nowadays, watch out for it because if the mouse is occupying your laptop's only serial port, you will not be able to use the PC for chart plotting or communications.

As with keyboards, wireless ones can be very useful and it is possible to buy combined keyboard/mouse wireless packages.

Although the idea of using a touch-screen is appealing, they often don't work well on board, for a number of reasons. Firstly, since your fingertip is often larger than the item you are trying to select on the screen, they can be inaccurate to use on a moving vessel. Secondly, depending upon the technology used, touch-screens can be ineffective with wet or damp fingers. Finally, and most importantly, many marine programs take advantage of the fact that mice typically have two buttons, using 'left-clicks' and 'right-clicks' to perform different tasks. A touch-screen is generally only able to provide a single click (usually interpreted by the software as a left-click). Some touch-screen manufacturers get around this by providing an on-screen button which when pressed means 'the next click is a right-click', but unless the marine software has been specifically designed around touch-screen limitations, it is likely to be pretty inconvenient to use on a regular basis.

Serial ports

The serial port on the PC is usually a 9-pin 'D' shaped connector (below left), although a few older PCs may be fitted with a 25-pin male 'D' connector (below right). Serial ports are often referred to as COM (for 'communication') ports and will be numbered, ie COM1, COM3, COM8 etc. You may also hear serial ports referred to as RS-232 ports, after the technical standard they are based on.

Serial ports are used extensively in marine computing for connecting the PC to navigation instruments, radio receivers, mobile phones etc. Until recently, most laptops had one serial port, most desktops two, which is fine for simple set-ups, but even so finding enough ports on the PC could be a problem in more complex systems.

Now, because of the increasing incidence of USB ports, infra-red and wireless communications, it is common for laptop computers to be shipped with no serial port fitted – this is obviously a problem for those whose navigation system will only 'talk to' a serial port.

A solution may be to add a serial to USB converter, or a PC Card with several serial ports fitted, but even then, you may run into problems involving limitations concerning the number and 'address' of serial ports fitted. Modern versions of Windows and marine software are much better than previous ones at working with serial ports, so it may be necessary to upgrade to get this to work. See chapter 12 Upgrading your PC.

The best option is to choose a PC that has a serial port fitted – there are still many models available that do.

Printer ports

Most PCs are fitted with one or two printer ports (usually one). Printer ports are also often called parallel ports because of the way data is transmitted using them. The connector on the PC is a 25-pin female 'D' shaped connector. The older 'Centronics' style connector used to be fitted to PCs as the printer port, but nowadays is only to be found on the printer itself.

25-pin printer port on the PC – note the holes, rather than pins

The printer port is much more flexible than its name suggests. As well as using it to connect the PC to a printer, a range of devices such as disc and tape drives and scanners can also be plugged in to the printer port. Most of these devices have a 'pass-through' capability, so a number of other devices could in theory be connected onto the same port; however, the use of a printer port for these devices normally means that speed is not as great as if they were connected to a SCSI, PCI or IDE card.

Many electronic chart manufacturers protect their charts against illegal copying through the use of a hardware 'security key' or

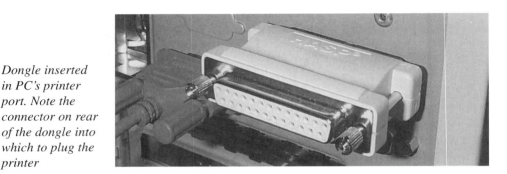

Dongle inserted in PC's printer port. Note the connector on rear of the dongle into which to plug the printer

'dongle' (see page 26). Most dongles take advantage of this pass-through capability and are connected to the PC using the printer port, allowing it to be used for a connection to a printer as well.

Unfortunately, some of the more modern printer drivers can cause problems when a dongle or another device wants to access the port, and the printer driver may need to be temporarily disabled. This is because some printer manufacturers ignore the Windows programming guidelines, and assume they are the only device using the port. This does not let other programs find their dongle or their hardware on the port, as the printer driver never lets their software look at the printer port.

USB ports

Historically, getting data into and out of a PC has relied on passing the data through a limited number of serial ports. Over the years, performance has not really kept up with processor development, so manufacturers have tried to develop devices to overcome the limitations of the humble serial port.

One such device is the Universal Serial Bus (USB) which looks to be able to deliver most of the benefits of serial ports, but at today's high speeds. Most computers shipped today, whether desktops or laptops, are equipped with USB, and since the technology allows many peripherals to be 'daisy-chained' together using just one port on the PC, USB should be particularly useful in the marine computing world. Though initially manufacturers were slow in creating peripherals that use USB, there are now many different devices (scanners, digital cameras, modems, printers etc) available.

In the early days, there were reliability problems with USB to serial converters, but thankfully as the technology matured, they became much more reliable and are a very useful way of connecting your PC's navigation software to your GPS or on-board instruments.

*PC Card half
inserted in its
slot. Most laptops
can take two
thinner cards or
one fatter one*

PC Cards (PCMCIA)

All laptops these days have two PC Card (formerly called PCMCIA) sockets. PC Card readers are also available for desktop-type PCs, although they are not very common. These credit card-sized cards slot into the sockets on the PC and give access to a wide range of extra hardware – for example, modems for a land line or mobile phone, or networking capabilities. Other add-ons include extra serial ports, sound and video capture cards etc. On board, their greatest uses are in adding extra serial ports, and for a fax/data card for a mobile phone.

Operating systems

The operating system is the interface between the program you want to run, and the computer's hardware. It lets you and your programs read and write to files, display things on the screen, print things out, and also often provides a common appearance and style of interaction between you and the PC.

If you buy a PC today it will generally be supplied with a version of Microsoft's Windows family installed. Earlier versions of Windows included the Windows 3 family; more recently the Windows 95, 98, Millenium Edition (ME) so called '16-bit' or 'Win 9x' family would have been supplied. Possibly, your PC may have been supplied with Windows NT (New Technology) or Windows 2000, more powerful (but more complex) 32-bit operating systems.

In 2001, Microsoft combined their 32-bit operating systems into the XP range. Although functionally pretty familiar to people used to working with the 9x or NT families, XP had a complete 'makeover' and was designed to complement the latest ultra-fast processors, to work better with a whole variety of peripherals (such as digital cameras, CD-R drives, DVD etc) and to make working with computer networks and the Internet much simpler.

Although under the same Windows brand name, it should be noted that Windows CE (or 'PocketPC') is a totally separate operating system from the rest of the Windows family. Applications written to operate under Windows CE on PDAs will not run under other versions of Windows, and vice versa.

Before Windows became common, most PCs used another much more basic operating system from Microsoft, called MS-DOS. This is nowadays part of computing history and though Microsoft offers a 'Command Prompt' option within Windows, it is unlikely that old MS-DOS software will run properly under these operating systems.

Another family of operating systems that runs on some PCs is based on Unix, which offered many of the facilities of Windows long before Windows came into existence. There are many variations of Unix – Solaris, Xenix, AIX and Linux to name a few. Whilst the public domain Linux is increasing in popularity, it requires considerably more expertise to install and run than Windows, and there is little available software for the marine market that runs under it. See also Appendix 1 Other Types of Personal Computer.

OK, so what should I buy?

With the rapid rate of PC development, you must accept that whatever you buy will be significantly cheaper within months of buying it. Also, if you want to buy leading edge technology you will pay a price premium – it is often worth staying one step back from the latest developments to enjoy large cost savings.

For an entry level system we would recommend the following minimum specification: 1.5 or 2 GHz CPU, 256Mb RAM, 20Gb hard disk, DVD-ROM drive with CD-R/CD-RW capability, Windows XP Home. The display should be a minimum of a 13.5" 1024x768 TFT display, with 16 Mb video RAM.

This should meet basic requirements for the next couple of years. If you want a machine with a longer life expectancy it's worth considering a marine PC, since with these, individual components can be upgraded as required.

When you have decided how powerful you want your PC to be, you still have to face the choice of what general type – laptop, office or marine PC – you want to have on board. This will often be obvious due to personal preference, your budget and the physical space available on your boat. You may, however, find the following of use in deciding the shape of 'the package' that you purchase.

Laptop

Most first-time users of PCs on board start with a laptop computer, and this statistic speaks for itself. Laptops have all their parts integrated onto a single board, giving a portable and compact system.

There are a some drawbacks with laptops: first, upgrading system components is seldom possible, and for repairs you are totally dependent on the length of time the manufacturer stocks spares. Secondly, it can be hard to expand a laptop because all you have is PC Card and USB slots, and peripherals of these types can be less versatile and more expensive than ISA or PCI slots. Finally, should the machine need repairing the machine will need sending back to the dealer for repairs.

Both laptop and marine PCs may have a place on board your vessel

The big advantages of a laptop are its small size and portability. When not sailing, you can easily whisk the machine off the boat and back to the home or office, and if you do not use the machine on board all of the time it can easily be stowed away in a locker.

Office PC

An office-type desktop or mini-tower PC has the CPU and the common peripherals all installed on a common board, the 'motherboard' or 'mainboard' (this typically encompasses the keyboard and mouse ports, serial and printer ports, USB port and IDE ports, together with expansion slots for AGP, PCI and IDE boards). Integrating these common elements makes the system cheap to produce, but a drawback is that if the motherboard needs repairs or maintenance, the whole PC will need to be dismantled; in fact, as prices fall, it is often cheaper and more convenient to replace the PC than to attempt to repair a motherboard.

PCs designed for home or office use are intended to be mounted in a static, upright position. Although the low price of such a computer makes it tempting to use on a boat, its design makes it vulnerable to damage from vibration and constant motion.

Marine PC

The marine PC is generally based on an industrial PC architecture. The key point here is that instead of using a motherboard, a 'passive backplane' is used. This consists of a simple baseboard with ISA and PCI bus expansion slots, with a combined PCI/ISA slot to allow the processor to be mounted on a card that is simply plugged in like any other expansion card. This makes it very easy to maintain, repair and upgrade the system.

The processor board generally has a minimum of the processor, memory, IDE ports, serial and parallel ports mounted on it. Depending on the system requirements, they can also be supplied with networking, SCSI bus and graphics card functionality all built in. This increased integration results in a saving in the number of boards required, which then results in a more compact machine.

Marine PCs generally have all of the components better secured than desktop machines, with shock mounted drives, and 12V or 24VDC power supplies. They may well be more compact than a typical desktop or mini-tower-type domestic PC and will usually be fitted with strong mounting lugs, so the unit may be securely fixed to the vessel (via shock-absorbing mountings).

Front panel of a typically robust marine PC

10 ■ Installing your PC

Using a PC on board is as straightforward as using one ashore; however, there are some special environmental factors that need to be considered when planning the installation. Also, power supply and interfacing requirements should be planned.

Planning the installation

There are a number of options when it comes to installing your PC, largely based on the hardware option you have chosen – whether a desktop, laptop or a marine PC.

Unfortunately, few boats are designed to take a laptop at the chart table, which is generally the most obvious place to site it. Assuming you do not have the space to mount it permanently, the best solution is to have a cradle built, or a drawer or 'letter box' slot that it can be kept in, preferably with all of the cables connected. Failing this, you will have the chore of disconnecting the cabling each time you want to stow the laptop away.

The best way to secure the laptop is often to use industrial strength Velcro strips underneath it, with the hooks on the laptop and the soft tape on the chart table. However, when doing this you need to ensure that you are not blocking any ventilation slots or covering up any of the catches found on many laptops.

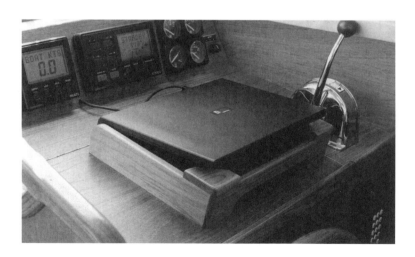

A particularly elegant 'cradle' designed to hold the laptop securely in place

If you have opted to have a separate display, keyboard and mouse connected to the laptop, installation is in many ways much easier. The laptop can be located out of the way in a locker or in the chart table, again secured with Velcro or a strap over the top; if you have a power switch mounted remotely then you will seldom need to access the laptop itself. With the low cost of TFT flat panel displays nowadays, this is a very popular solution – and still allows you to take your PC home when you leave the boat. The only points to watch are that the locker must not be damp, and must have reasonable ventilation.

Marine PCs are designed to be easy to install; most are supplied with mounting rails to secure them in place. As with a laptop, a marine PC needs to be located in a compartment with ventilation holes that does not get too hot – the recommended maximum internal operating temperature is about 55° C, and the PC will generally run about 10° warmer than the surrounding air. On a marine PC, cooling fans are normally filtered to minimise dust ingress, so the filters will need cleaning or replacing periodically.

Screens and keyboards

When deciding on where to locate a flat screen display, consideration needs to be given to its viewing characteristics. TFT displays can typically be read at angles of up to 60°–80° off centre each side, and 10°–20° up and down. If angles greater than this are required, then you may want to mount the display on an adjustable tilt and swivel mount. If the screen has a reflective surface, you will also need to minimise glare from reflected lights.

The other major consideration with a display is its brightness. Below decks, or protected from bright light, a display with a brightness of 150–300 candela/m^2 (or NITS) will be adequate, but in bright light or direct sunlight a brightness of 1000 candela/m^2 will be required to allow the screen to be read in direct light. Also, consideration needs to be given to the screen's ability to be dimmed down, for if it cannot be dimmed right down then it should not be mounted in the line of vision of the helmsman or other crew members on watch at night.

The screen needs to be connected to the video output of the PC with good-quality video cable – too poor a quality and there will be 'ghosting', shown by text looking as though it has a shadow to it. For cable runs over about 15 metres, a video booster will be needed. With higher-quality laptops, the screen can run at a differ-

Here, in a well-designed navigation area, the marine PC is given pride of place

ent resolution from the laptop's screen, but with many the two must run at the same resolution, so you will need to match the screen to the laptop.

The keyboard and pointing device can either be console mounted, with a keyboard and trackball let into the surface of the chart table, or left free on the top. If console mounted, keyboards and mice should be mounted on a near horizontal surface – when operating them on vertical surfaces one's hand is cocked up at an impracticable and uncomfortable angle.

With separate keyboards and mice, the cables can be broken so as to have sockets at the rear of the chart table to plug the actual devices into. Instead of a mouse, consider a trackball secured to the chart table with the ubiquitous Velcro, as this will not roll around with the boat's movement. Alternatively, with a cordless keyboard and mouse the items can simply be placed in a drawer when not in use, but if the link is infra-red then there must be no obstructions when in use, or if it is a radio link then there must be no metal obstructions.

Environmental considerations

It is possible to purchase completely ruggedised and waterproofed equipment, built to tough military standards, but of course this is rarely within the budget of the typical yachtsman. However, by addressing the major environmental enemies of electronic equipment on board a seagoing vessel, and taking other commonsense precautions, it is perfectly reasonable to anticipate a long and reliable life from most modern PCs on board.

Shock and vibration

The insides of a computer, and its disk drive, are generally much more shock resistant than most people realise, and on most boats no special precautions need to be taken. On a well designed marine PC, designed with a configuration that anticipates high shock loadings, expansion and motherboards are mounted vertically; if it uses a Pentium processor this will be mounted parallel to its processor board, as opposed to the normal right angle mounting on domestic PCs.

For high-speed vessels or those operating in very harsh conditions, the PC can be mounted on anti-shock mounts, which will also help to avoid vibration problems. Regardless of how the PC is mounted, the CD-ROM drive and floppy disk drive will not operate well in severe conditions, so it is wise to have all important programs and data (charts etc) loaded onto the PC before you encounter these conditions.

Vibration can be a more insidious problem, with the potential for components to slowly work loose with time. Whilst all internal boards in a PC have a retaining screw at one end, in a marine PC the whole board is held down by a retaining strap and guide over the boards at the other end, locking everything in place. Also, installation details such as having cables to the PC secured down will help avoid their shaking loose. Most customers prefer to avoid nonstandard screw-in or lock-in cable connectors being used, as these increase costs and mean that standard PC cables and components cannot be used.

Temperature

The maximum operating temperature of most PC components is typically about 55–60° C. You may think that your equipment will not reach this temperature, but because it is air cooled it requires the surrounding air to be 10° C cooler or more. Because of this, it is essential that the equipment is mounted in a vented locker, and that fans and air vents are not blocked. Whilst a good-quality marine PC can monitor its internal temperature, and in some cases also generate a high temperature alarm, with other equipment you are relying on good installation practice.

If the equipment is mounted where it is exposed to sunlight, then heating from solar radiation can also be significant. The heating effect will be at a maximum in the tropics, when the sun is usually high above the horizon, and the exposed surface may be at right angles to the sun's rays. It is also more of a problem for components with a dark matt finish, fitted in a metal casing with high thermal conductivity.

LCD displays have their own particular problems in temperature extremes. At sub-zero temperatures the display may initially fail to operate, though they normally heat up quickly. At very high temperatures the display may black out, particularly when heated by the sun. This can be solved by gently cooling it with seawater, or by strategically placing a crew member to keep it in the shade.

It should also be noted that if LCDs are operated at high temperatures, this will also have a long term effect of shortening the life of the panel (it will rapidly become dim with age). High temperature problems are particularly likely to occur with high brightness displays that are not fitted with a cooling fan, since the backlight and electronics output a lot of heat into a small enclosed space, which will overheat on deck when exposed to warm weather and a bright sun.

Humidity

Humidity on its own can cause problems with condensation forming and shorting out components, connections or wires, but when coupled with a salt atmosphere, salt crystals in the air are deposited on the components and cause additional corrosion. Laptops are particularly prone to these problems, because having everything compressed into such a small place means that connectors are relatively small and more prone to corrosion problems. Also, they do not have the filtered fans of a marine PC, so it is easier for salt crystals in the atmosphere to enter the PC. However, with almost all computer equipment the motherboards are coated to protect against corrosion.

Apart from keeping the boat's atmosphere as dry as possible, a useful tip is to keep equipment running continuously when on board, keeping a constant working temperature inside the unit.

When the PC is switched off it cools down, encouraging salty, corrosive condensation to form. When switched back on, the increase in temperature makes this condensation more corrosive until it has evaporated off.

Power supply

Running a PC on board requires both a good-quality and reliable power source. In fact, the power source is at least as important as the PC, which will be useless unless it has sufficient electrical power to run.

There are various methods of supplying power to your PC while your vessel is under way, but some methods may not be as effective or electrically efficient as others.

Internal computer batteries

All laptop and notebook PCs have interchangeable, rechargeable batteries. Until recently, one could expect fairly short running times of around an hour or two. However, significant improvements in power storage technology have greatly extended operating times to around four or five hours in a typical laptop. This is even the case with today's large, high resolution, bright TFT screens that are notoriously power-hungry.

Four or five hours of operation is fine for an occasional day sail, especially if fully charged spare batteries are kept close to hand. Yachtsmen who rely on their PC for navigation, however, will require longer operating times and therefore will either need several spares or a method of charging the PC's internal batteries whilst away from shore power.

DC-DC converters

Various DC-DC converters are commercially available. These are generally made up of a cigarette lighter attachment and a plug to fit into the PC's DC power socket. They operate by converting the boat's 12VDC or 24VDC supply to the operating voltage of the PC. When laptop PCs first became common, suitable DC-DC converters were hard to find, but as the market for laptops has expanded, many branded as well as after-market units are available, aimed mainly at the executive with a company car.

Whilst ideal for in-car use, DC-DC converters suffer a number of drawbacks in the marine environment:

- Most DC-DC converters only provide DC power to the PC to operate it, they do not charge the batteries at the same time. This is significant since the PC's internal batteries can provide a valuable 'get you home' safety margin, should the boat's DC supply fail (assuming you also have spare batteries for your GPS set!).

- DC-DC converters bypass the PC's own power supply unit (PSU) and provide DC power directly to the PC's motherboard. In the event of a high voltage spike from the yacht's electrical system or a fault occurring in the converter itself, the motherboard may get damaged. If a non-manufacturer-approved DC-DC converter has been used, this will almost certainly invalidate the PC's warranty.
- The method of connection to the yacht's electrical system is not very reliable – usually, a cigar lighter socket or similar is used and this may not have a fuse of a suitable rating fitted.
- DC-DC converters are not always available in 24VDC for commercial or larger boat use.
- Some DC-DC converters may cause interference to weatherfax and weathersat reception

DC to AC power inverters

Inverters convert 12 or 24VDC power from the boat's batteries to 230VAC mains electricity. This allows the PC to operate in exactly the same way as if it were plugged into the mains at home. If you are using a laptop PC, an inverter is certainly the preferred option because it provides valuable charging of the PC's own batteries. In any case, having an inverter on board allows the use of other AC devices such as printers, mobile phones, VHF radio chargers etc. It may even be cheaper to buy an inverter than several 'car chargers'.

> **Warning –** Inverters produce AC electrical power at 120–240V. **This is sufficient to kill** and is more hazardous than dealing with 12 or 24VDC electrical power on board. There are also many different inverter technologies available, so care must be taken to ensure that a suitable inverter is chosen. Unless you are familiar with marine electrics, this is an area where it is usually best to consult with an expert before purchasing an inverter.

Efficiency

On a boat with limited power generation capability, it is extremely important that losses of electrical energy are kept to an absolute minimum. This has traditionally been a reason for not using an inverter, since older models were notoriously inefficient. Happily, the situation is now much better, with most inverter manufacturers quoting efficiency percentages in the mid nineties. With a modern, correctly installed inverter, there is no reason why the yachtsman can't have a reasonable quantity of good-quality AC power available on board at all times.

What size inverter?

As a rough guide, the following sizes of inverter should be used for different PCs:

Inverter size	Type of PC	Other Uses
75–150W	Notebook	Bubblejet printer, mobile phone/VHF charger
250–500W	Desktop/Marine	As above + televisions and small power tools
1000–2000W	As above	Laser printer, plotter and most domestic appliances

If planning to use an inverter in excess of 150W it is essential to check the yacht's DC electrical system and battery capacity to ensure they are capable of coping with the electrical load that would result from using the inverter at full power. Such an inverter should be placed on its own DC electrical circuit and be protected with a suitably rated fuse and/or breaker.

Modified v pure sine-wave inverters

There are essentially two types of AC electrical output produced by inverters; these are known as modified (or stepped, quasi or trapezoidal) sine-wave and pure sine-wave.

AC electricity, when plotted on a graph, gives a smooth wave shape that looks rather like a radio wave. Modified sine-wave units attempt to provide a similar-looking waveform with a number of steps up and back down again. Laptop and desktop PCs will usually operate well from a modified sine-wave inverter. However, a pure sine-wave inverter is often required for many specialist, and even some 'standard', PC monitors.

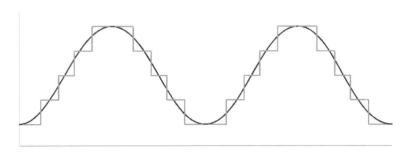

Modified sine-wave inverters attempt to model a pure sine-wave in small steps

The table below compares modified and pure sine-wave inverters:

	Pure Sine	Modified Sine
Cost	*	*****
Operating efficiency	*****	****
Running notebooks	*****	****
Running desktops	*****	*
Running bubblejet printer	*****	****
Running laser printers	*****	*
Interference	*****	*
Running other peripherals	*****	****

Key: 1 * = poor, 5 * = excellent

In fact, when choosing an inverter, it is not as simple as deciding between modified or pure sine-wave output, because there are also three types of power conversion technology used in inverters. The power conversion technology used has a great bearing on the efficiency, life and interference produced by the inverter – as well, of course, as on its cost.

It may help to understand the benefits and drawbacks of the main conversion technologies:

1 Ferroresonant
This type of inverter uses a large transformer and fairly basic circuitry to provide AC power. Such inverters are generally very reliable but are not recommended for use on boats as their efficiency is poor.

2 Switch mode
This type of inverter is much smaller, lighter and efficient than other units. Most switch mode inverters are of the modified sine-wave type. They are ideal for marine use; however, they are not as reliable as ferroresonant types and can produce interference if not installed correctly.

3 Hybrid
The latest inverter technology combines a hybrid transformer with a switch-mode design. These are much more reliable than switch-mode units and produce less interference. They are often more expensive than ferroresonant and switch mode units and generally produce a pure sine-wave.

A small inverter may be powerful enough for a laptop PC

In summary, inverters are the preferred method of providing power for laptop PCs. A modern laptop PC with fairly modest power requirements can be driven from a 75W inverter, not much larger than a packet of cigarettes, though some more powerful machines may require a 150W inverter.

If you have a desktop or marine PC on board, you will probably need a larger inverter, at least 250W. This is where there is the greatest choice in terms of output waveforms and power conversion technology available and, given a suitable DC electrical system to back it up, a larger inverter can be used to power many other devices on board as well as a PC.

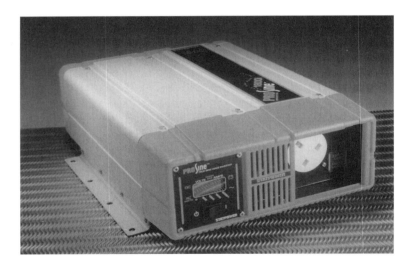

A more powerful unit will be required for desktop and marine PCs

If you have a well specified DC system on board, maybe with a separate 'navigation system' battery circuit, it is quite feasible to dispense with an inverter, to avoid the associated electrical losses. With desktop or marine PCs, it is usually possible to have the built-in 240VAC power supply unit replaced with a 12 or 24VDC unit.

Interference

One of the less welcome aspects of DC-AC power inverters can be electrical interference, which may interrupt radio reception and in some extreme cases cause problems with screen visibility. Produced as a by-product of the DC-AC conversion, waste energy is given off as heat (which is why larger inverters have 'heat sink' fins and must be sited correctly) as well as interference.

Coping with electrical interference on small boats can be a bit of a 'black art', but common remedies include: moving the inverter away from the PC, other electrics, instruments or wires that carry signals; orienting the inverter differently; fitting 'chokes' around video and signal cables.

The best way to avoid dealing with interference on board is to stop it happening in the first place. To this end, it is worth consulting a professional or asking a supplier for a trial unit before committing to a purchase. Generally though, most modern, pure sine-wave, hybrid units will produce acceptably small levels of electrical interference which can be dealt with by siting and installing the inverter sensibly.

Batteries and power generation

Whether running your PC through an inverter or direct from the boat's 12 or 24VDC supply, one thing is certain: you will wish you had bigger batteries!

It has been common practice for some years now for boats to have separate battery circuits for domestic power requirements and for engine starting. The obvious reason is that there should always be electrical power available to start the boat's engine, even if the domestic batteries are drained.

In a similar way, as yachtsmen become more and more reliant on electronics, there is a definite trend for on-board electrical systems to become more powerful and more 'bullet-proof'. Indeed, it is not uncommon nowadays to see new boats equipped with three battery banks, intended for domestic power, engine start and, last but not least, critical navigation systems.

If you are planning to use your PC for navigation, especially chart plotting, or if you have many electronic navigation aids on board, you may consider fitting a separate battery and even a separate charging system, to ensure that these systems can be relied upon.

If you do fit extra battery capacity, you should also consider upgrading your charging capacity, maybe by fitting a bigger, or second, alternator, or a solar or wind charging system.

Uninterruptible power supplies (UPS)

You may consider fitting an uninterruptible power supply (UPS) to avoid your PC restarting if the electrical supply is interrupted or the voltage drops too low. If using an external UPS, it must be run off a 240VAC mains power supply (note if using an inverter it must be a true sine-wave inverter since other inverters will trip the UPS with each cycle, leaving it ticking like a clock as it trips in and out). Alternatively a UPS can be fitted inside a DC-powered marine PC, but the drawback with this is that it will only protect the processor unit and not the display in the event of a power outage.

Basic UPSs provide a fairly limited 'autonomy' from their internal batteries in the event of a power failure. This autonomy is intended to allow the PC to shut down 'gracefully' (by closing down programs in the correct sequence), not as an alternative means of operation. UPSs with significant autonomy (more than a couple of minutes) are not only very expensive, but also extremely heavy, being comprised of large, usually lead-acid, batteries.

Remote displays and workstations

Some users wish to display computer information remotely, or to operate the PC from a different part of the boat. Examples of this are having the chart plotter repeated to a screen up on deck, or having a PC shared between the saloon and the master cabin.

A video splitter can split the PC output to a number of repeater displays, at the same time boosting the signal strength to support longer cable runs. Alternatively a switch box can be used to equip some or all of these repeat stations with a keyboard and mouse, allowing full remote operation of the equipment.

There may also be a requirement to connect the PC together with an on board TV or video, to show computer output on the TV, or TV programmes on the PC monitor. Generally, these kinds of installation are best left to the professionals.

Anyone for television?

As television becomes more popular on small boats, finding space for both a computer display and TV screen can be challenging. When one considers that they are rarely used simultaneously, it can make sense to use the same screen for both purposes.

Outputting the PC display to a TV screen is relatively easy, with the video signal being provided by a TV converter (either an add-on, or built into the PC), and a modulator if necessary to change the TV channel used for the computer display. However, the resolution of a TV screen is much lower than a computer screen, so some loss of image quality may be experienced. Also, taking higher resolution PC output to a TV can be very expensive.

It is generally better to go the other route – fit a TFT flat screen PC monitor and convert the TV signal (PAL, NTSC or SECAM) to a computer signal. This can be done with a separate converter box, and the monitor can then be switched between TV and PC output as required.

Even better, with a marine PC, a TV expansion board can be fitted, which allows the TV image to be displayed in a window on the monitor or as a full screen image (as well as offering the facility to record video clips or still images for those so inclined). For the increasing number of PCs that are fitted with a DVD drive, you get the ability to play DVD films over the TV system as well – much more compact and reliable than video-cassettes. At present DVD players are designed to be locked into one of four world regions (they only play DVD discs from one region, to avoid customers buying cheaper videos from other regions); however, software tools are available to unlock the players and, in any case, multi-region DVD drives are becoming available.

Important Note – For those planning to travel greater distances, a word of caution is required concerning different TV and video signal formats. In the USA, TV signals conform to the NTSC standard, but this is not used in Europe where there are a number of versions of the PAL standard (PAL-I for the UK, and PAL B/G for most of southern Europe for example), and France uses its own SECAM format. Some TVs and videos will only work with the one format, while others will support either the range of PAL formats or NTSC, and a very few will support all formats.

Using a computer display connected to a PC with a TV expansion board would seem to be the route offering the widest range of options; however, this does mean that all TV viewing would have to be done through the PC.

11 ▪ Interfacing Your PC

Interfacing – the theory

Back in the early days of marine electronics, each piece of equipment was a stand-alone unit that could not communicate with the outside world. However, manufacturers quickly recognised that it would make sense if instruments could send and receive information to each other, and began designing instruments which could 'communicate'.

These new instrument systems were far more powerful than had been possible with stand-alone instruments – imagine how useful it is, for example, to be able to automatically work out the true wind speed and direction, given input from the log, compass and an apparent wind sensor.

This idea quickly caught on, but with the significant drawback that if a customer owned instruments from different manufacturers, it was extremely unlikely that these instruments would be able to 'talk' to each other. This is because each manufacturer used its own private or 'proprietary' communications language.

NMEA 0183

In the early 1980s in the USA, the NMEA (National Marine Electronics Association) formed a communications standard intended to allow equipment from different manufacturers to communicate easily, with obvious benefits to the consumer.

The original standard went through a number of developments, but stabilised at the NMEA0183 standard. The result is that nowadays almost all instruments can send (and often receive) NMEA0183 data, even if manufacturers use their own proprietary communications system between their own instruments. Though the NMEA0183 specification is updated periodically to keep pace with new developments, it is 'backwardly-compatible' so newer equipment should always be able to send and receive NMEA0183 data that older compatible equipment can use.

At its most basic level, NMEA0183 communications consist of a 'talker' sending out data in 'sentences' to one or more 'listeners'. The talker does this regardless of whether or not a listener is connected, and in fact has no way of knowing if any other equipment is actually receiving the data.

This is an extremely powerful facility – NMEA0183 makes it possible to connect your PC to a wide variety of on-board instruments and for software running on your PC to receive and use information the instruments transmit.

> **Tip** – Most people refer to the NMEA0183 specification as 'NEMA 183' which, although inaccurate, is phonetically far more convenient!

Electrical signals

It's important to note that NMEA0183 is not just a 'language', it actually consists of a full specification defining electrical signal levels as well as the format of the data to be used.

With NMEA0183 data is sent down a pair of wires, officially named A and B, but more usually called signal (+) and ground (–) or similar. A great deal of effort went into specifying a system that can travel long distances in an electrically noisy environment without becoming corrupted. The signal is 'differential' in that the logical status 'on' or 'off' is defined by the *difference* between the voltages on the signal and ground wires, rather than an absolute voltage. This means that electrical interference is minimised. Note that the voltage levels may be anything from 2V to 15V, well outside of the range in the PC's serial port RS232 specification, though the use of a proper NMEA/RS232 converter will ensure that voltages are converted to and from the RS232 and NMEA0183 specifications.

Opto-isolation

As part of the NMEA specification, the listener device must be opto-isolated. At its simplest, this means that the incoming signal switches a bulb on and off, and the listener detects the state of the bulb. Just having on and off states for the bulb is another tool in the fight against interference, and the lack of a direct physical connection also minimises the risk of damage from voltage surges down the line.

Data format

NMEA0183 data can consist of a wide range of sentences, each with their own meaning, most of which are part of the specification and all use a common format.

```
$GPRMC,153334,A,5051.64,N,00117.70,W,005.0,131.5,100295,004.3,W*7D
$GPRMB,A,0.00,L,,NAB,5040.05,N,00057.07,W,017.5,131.5,005.0,V*68
$GPR00,NAB,,,,,,,,,,,,*08
$GPGLL,5051.64,N,00117.70,W*7A
$PGRMZ,-212,f,3*37
$GPXTE,A,A,0.00,L,N*6E
$GPBWC,153335,5040.05,N,00057.07,W,131.5,T,135.8,M,017.5,N,NAB*55
$GPRMC,153336,A,5051.64,N,00117.70,W,005.0,131.5,100295,004.3,W*7F
$GPRMB,A,0.00,L,,NAB,5040.05,N,00057.07,W,017.5,131.5,005.0,V*68
$GPWPL,5040.05,N,00057.07,W,NAB*15
$GPGLL,5051.64,N,00117.70,W*7A
$PGRMZ,-212,f,3*37
$GPXTE,A,A,0.00,L,N*6E
$GPBWC,153337,5040.05,N,00057.07,W,131.5,T,135.8,M,017.5,N,NAB*57
$GPRMC,153338,A,5051.64,N,00117.70,W,005.0,131.5,100295,004.3,W*71
```

NMEA0183 sentences have a standard structure

Each sentence begins with a $ sign, then the next two characters identify the type of equipment sending the data. Next, three letters define the type of data that is held in the rest of the sentence. After this comes the data itself, with each item separated by a comma. At the end there may be an * followed by two characters. This is an optional checksum, which the listener can use to check whether the sentence has been corrupted in its transmission. See the diagram above which shows typical NMEA0183 sentences.

There are also manufacturer's proprietary sentences that begin with $P and then the manufacturer's ID, which can hold anything the manufacturer decides. Equipment normally transmits data in a sequence, with each sentence being repeated every one or two seconds (though this may be much more frequent).

Generally, this is straightforward and works pretty well in most cases, but because the standard has developed on a fairly *ad-hoc* basis, there can be some problems:

- First, a listener can decide which sentences (and even which parts of the sentence) it will interpret (or listen out for). This means that two NMEA0183 devices may not communicate at all if the talker is not outputting anything the listener understands.

- Secondly, the talker can decide not only which sentences to output, but it can also decide not to fill in all of the data in a sentence, and just leave some of it blank (though there are a few sentences where it is mandatory for all fields to be completed).

- Finally, for common items such as vessel position and depth the talker often can choose from a wide range of sentences, each providing similar (but not identical) information. Because of this, it is worth checking with manufacturers or suppliers whether or not pieces of equipment will talk to each other.

Whilst it is generally acknowledged that it is not perfect, the NMEA0183 format has allowed a wide variety of instruments to work together, and any problems have tended to affect instrument manufacturers and installers more than end users.

NMEA0183 troubleshooting

Usually, NMEA0183 interfacing is quite straightforward and is simply a matter of methodically following manufacturers' instructions. Sometimes, though, you may experience problems. If you do, the following may prove useful:

If you are having trouble receiving or just want to look at NMEA0183 data, one of the easiest ways is to use the *Hyperterminal* software included with Windows 95, 98, Millenium Edition and XP. If you do not have this installed, any Windows-based communications package will do.

1 Confirm that the NMEA0183 device is switched on and set up to transmit data, by referring to its installation or user guide (some hand-held GPS sets won't export unless connected to an external 12VDC supply, using the manufacturer-supplied cable).

2 Set *Hyperterminal* up (serial port number usually COM1 or COM2, data rate 4800 bps, 8 data bits, 1 stop bit, no parity and no flow control), and when you connect the instrument(s) to the serial port you chose, you should see the NMEA0183 data streaming in. This input can be saved to disk or printed off, which can help manufacturers diagnose NMEA0183 incompatibilities.

If nothing appears in the *Hyperterminal* screen, you can use a voltmeter (set to DC Volts) across the A and B lines from the NMEA0183 device, and you should see the voltage fluctuate up and down as data passes down the line. If you see nothing, suspect a faulty or badly wired cable and double check that the GPS is set up to export data. Sometimes swapping the A and B lines over may solve problems.

Splitting and combining NMEA0183 signals

Because NMEA0183 data is simply broadcast by the talker, its output can be split to a number of listeners. In many cases you can divide the wires at a junction box, but sooner or later the electrical load imposed by each listener on the talker becomes too much, and the signal breaks down. If this happens, you'll need a proper *expansion box* or *booster* that will increase the driver current available. The load of each listener, and the current available at each talker, can vary significantly, and there is no certain way of telling in advance whether a distribution box/booster will be required.

Sooner or later you will encounter the reverse problem – you want to combine data from a number of talkers into a device which may have just one listener port. For this you need a *multiplexer*, which is fitted with a number of listeners (usually four) and one talker. Incoming data on each listener port is held until a complete sentence is received and is then transmitted on the talker port. If the four inputs are all busy then their total input may well exceed the capacity of the talker, and some sentences may be dropped periodically. However, as almost all data is transmitted on a regular basis by the instruments, this seldom causes a problem.

If you need to multiplex more than four signals together it is possible to 'daisy-chain' NMEA0183 multiplexers together – ie connecting the output of a four-input multiplexer into one of the inputs of another similar multiplexer, thus obtaining seven inputs. If you plan to do this, please heed the advice above concerning exceeding the capacity of the talkers. Some multiplexers will get around this by setting the talker port up to transmit data at 9600 baud (twice as fast as standard NMEA0183), but make sure that the PC program you are using can receive NMEA0183 data at 9600 baud.

NMEA0183 signals may be easily split, combined and boosted for more complex installations

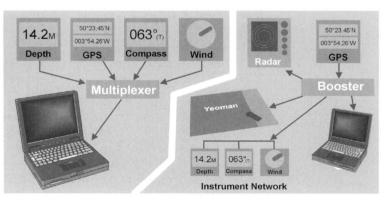

NMEA 2000 – the future of instrument interfacing?

Various versions of the NMEA0183 interface have been almost universal for some years now, but it has become increasingly stretched in terms of the amount of data it can carry; it is also not ideally suited to connecting many devices together.

The National Marine Electronics Association (of America) is finalising details of a new protocol called NMEA2000, which is designed to overcome these limitations. NMEA2000 is designed to run on the CAN bus which was originally developed for the automotive industry – this allows equipment manufacturers to use standard and well-tried components which, due to economies of scale, are low in cost.

The new system is based on a single cable carrying both power and data to all components attached to it – they are simply 'teed off' where required. This gets around the problems of 'talkers' and 'listeners' which the NMEA0183 standard is based on, and saves having to run separate DC wires to some equipment. NMEA2000 will also be much faster than NMEA0183, achieved using a higher physical data rate and a very compact binary data format.

NMEA2000 has also allowed the designers to start with a clean sheet of paper and given them a chance to sort out redundancy and incompatibilities of data sentences which crept in as NMEA0183 developed over the years.

There will of course be drawbacks – for large yachts and commercial vessels the maximum length of the system (which is governed by signal timing requirements) could be a problem. But these kinds of potential problems can be overcome by the use of junction boxes (similar to 'routers' in a normal PC network).

Other interfacing technologies are emerging which may suit the commercial marine world, but, designed for military uses, these are likely to be too expensive for widespread leisure marine use.

Wired networks

An increasing number of boats are fitting a small Ethernet local area network (LAN) on board. For example, if they have a main PC and a laptop, this lets them share files and printers and other devices between computers, and it also can allow either machine to access the Internet independently.

Simply put, each computer on the network is attached with special network cables to a network 'hub' which deals with network communication.

Network hubs are nowadays very inexpensive and easy to install – indeed many of them run on 12VDC. Networking is almost universally to the 100Mb/s CAT 5 standard, though it is better to use shielded cabling (STP) rather then the unshielded cabling (UTP) often used in offices.

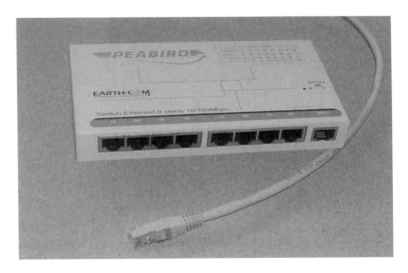

A low-cost 8-port network hub

Having a network on board can simplify NMEA interfacing by using a network interface box. This makes NMEA data available to any PC on the network and can make installation much easier by minimising cable runs. A small network interface box plugs into the network hub in exactly the same way as a PC would, and may have four ports on it to accept up to four NMEA interfaces – of course, any number of these could be installed as required.

Once the NMEA data is 'on the network' it can easily be passed around to the software that requires it.

Wireless networks

Whilst a wired network can be very convenient on board, and well within the means and capabilities of the average yachtsman to achieve, some boats are doing away with wires to link the PC network together and are instead using a Wireless LAN.

The network hub and each PC's network adapter function as short-range radio transceivers, allowing network data to be transmitted between the PCs wirelessly.

This may be to the 802.11b 'WiFi' standard, or to the newly emerging and faster 802.11a standard (still undergoing approval for use in Europe at the time of writing).

A wireless network can be very convenient if you are using laptops on board, but the structure on many boats means that the range is much less than in open air.

A wireless network should normally be set up by a professional – if the network is not configured properly there could be security issues, allowing the neighbouring boat to log onto your network.

Infra red

Though not strictly speaking networking, many laptop PCs have an infra red communication port built in. A typical use for a yachtsman would be to communicate with a mobile phone for e-mail, but even some portable printers can use it as well.

Again the benefit to the user is that no wires are needed. However, because you need to point an infra red device at another for them to communicate, at sea the devices inevitably slide about and lose communication. In general we would recommend using a cable or radio-based system instead.

12 ▪ Upgrade Your PC?

In a field as fast moving as computing, equipment purchased can become obsolete pretty quickly and it sometimes seems as if there is a conspiracy between hardware and software manufacturers to force people to upgrade more quickly than they would want.

Here's how it goes: your existing laptop's hard disk is getting full and it is running pretty slowly, what with all the software you have loaded onto it over the last couple of years. You want to get a new electronic charting program, but you know you'll need more disk space for the charts, and suspect you'll need a faster processor to handle all the graphics. Should you buy another laptop?

Upgrade, replace or tidy

Well, before you rush down to the computer shop, take a moment to consider your options.

Firstly, is your disk really full? It's worth taking the time to establish this as often some simple disk housekeeping can free up an astonishing amount of space. Are there any large files you can archive off because you use them infrequently? Are there any programs on your PC that you no longer use? What about that heavyweight 'Office type' suite of programs that was installed on the PC when you bought it, but which you've never used?

If your PC doesn't already have one, it may be worth investing in a CD-writer (external for laptops, internal for desktops) and backing-up these files onto CD-R discs. For unused or infrequently used programs, as long as you still have the original distribution discs, use Windows' Add/Remove programs tool to uninstall them.

Once you've liberated some space, try running Windows' Disk Cleanup and then the Disk Defragmenter utility to clear some more.

You may even wipe or 'reformat' your hard disk. This option is not for the faint-hearted however – make sure you have backed up all your important data and have original distribution discs and any necessary codes to reinstall software from. Get a quote from your local computer company to do this if unsure.

The chances are that you've freed up enough disk space now, but surely a new machine will be much faster, won't it?

Technically, yes. But the shiny new laptop at the computer store will probably have a later version of Windows running on it than you are using at the moment. As well as being more powerful, new operating systems are almost always bigger and more bloated than their ancestors and you may find that even though the new machine has a faster processor, much of the benefit of this is lost to running that new operating system. Ignore the marketing men – resist new operating systems!

If you haven't already done so, check how much RAM memory your existing PC has fitted, and how much you can add until it is full. Adding more RAM is the single most effective way of improving your PC's performance. And as memory prices continue to fall, it's cheap too.

Most laptops have two slots for SODIMM memory, concealed by a plate on the underside

The above are good strategies for extending the life of an older laptop PC – in fact they are pretty much the only things you can do to a laptop anyway, but desktops and marine PCs offer a more flexible upgrade situation because you can improve other parts as well, like video cards and processors etc.

However, bear in mind that any PC is a system, comprised of a collection of components that are matched so as to avoid bottlenecks. To add a huge fast hard disk and loads of memory to your old desktop PC could be a false economy unless you consider changing the video card, processor and motherboard as well – in fact, many consider basic desktop PCs so inexpensive that they are not cost-effective to upgrade – they simply budget to replace them every couple of years.

Appendix 1 ▪ Other Types of Personal Computer

Since the vast majority of computers used aboard boats conform to the definition in chapter 1, this book has focused on them. However, just so you don't miss out, and because one of the following may be more suitable for your needs, here is a brief description of other computers you might consider using:

Programmable calculators

These were the first type of computer used aboard leisure boats, as early as the 1970s. They offered the navigator a small device capable of calculating simple mathematical functions. Since they didn't have much memory for storing data, the user would have to type in the required data and the calculator would run a small built-in sequence of mathematical operations on the data, presenting a numerical output which the user would then use in the traditional navigation process. Some models require the user to type in the 'programs' as well, having no way of storing this information when the unit is switched off.

Whilst programmable calculators are necessarily limited in their use, various manufacturers have enhanced the programs running on them and they can now store more 'user data'. They offer the benefits of relatively low cost, small size and low power consumption and are suited to the maths involved in astro navigation, thus they are quite common amongst blue-water sailors.

There are also some programmable calculators offering simple tidal calculations and even those that have a sufficiently large screen to draw a tidal curve in a graphical format.

Although programmable computers are not usually waterproof, water-resistant pouches to protect them are available.

PDAs

Personal Digital Assistants or PDAs are also known as palmtop computers by virtue of their small size. They are much more powerful than programmable calculators and, as well as the built-in programs, you can add a range of programs to extend their use.

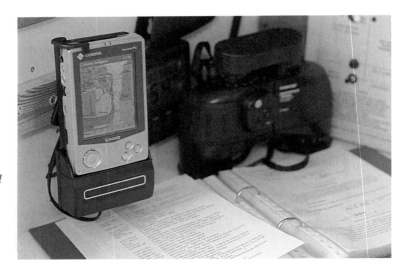

Sometimes limited by small screens, PDAs can nevertheless be very useful on board

PDAs are a 'halfway house' between programmable calculators and PCs – relatively inexpensive, very small, and again using little electrical power. They can do a lot more than the calculators, and though smaller models can be limited, many now have colour screens which are large and sharp enough to be able to display electronic charts or other graphical information conveniently.

In the past, each brand of PDA utilised its own operating system, and this meant that programs written for a particular model would rarely function properly, if at all on a different model.

However in recent years, the situation has changed for the better and the introduction of a simplified version of Microsoft Windows, originally called Windows CE, then PocketPC has made it worth while for developers to produce software that will run on many PDAs, not just one model.

Many of the mainstream PC manufacturers – Hewlett-Packard, Compaq, Sony etc, produce PocketPC PDAs, and other manufacturers, such as Casio (PocketPC) and Palm (PalmOS) have good market penetration with several models available.

As PDAs have developed over the last few years, they have tended to become larger and offer facilities more like normal laptop computers, at the same time as laptops are getting smaller and are described as ultralight laptops or notebook computers. Though this trend is likely to continue, the important distinction is that laptops are very much like traditional PC, only smaller. PDAs on the other hand, are designed from the ground up to be operated primarily by touching the screen with finger or a special pen, rather than with a keyboard.

Again, palmtops are not usually waterproof, although there are waterproof cases available to fit them.

The Apple Macintosh

The 'Mac', like the PC, is also a 'real computer', capable of doing everything you are likely to want to do with a PC on board. Indeed it is often argued in the computer press that Macs are better designed and easier to use than PCs. Both 'camps' have strong followings and users have been known to get very animated over why their favourite is 'best'.

The reality is that whilst it is hard to say that either type is better or worse than the other, market activity over the last few years has resulted in there being an awful lot more PCs on desks than Macs.

So what does this mean for yachtsmen? Ultimately if you own a PC, there will be a far greater choice of programs to choose from than those written specifically for Macs.

This does not mean that Macintosh users have no choices at all; there are some excellent marine programs that have been written for the Mac and an owner may also be able to run PC software on their Mac through the use of an 'emulator' program (see below).

If a Macintosh owner can't find suitable marine software written for their Mac, it's worth pointing out that PCs are now so inexpensive that Mac owners have been known to purchase a laptop PC simply to gain access to the marine software system of their choice.

Windows emulators for the Macintosh

Internally, the Macintosh is very different from a regular IBM compatible PC, this is why they use their own operating system, called System X (where X is the current version, eg System 8, 9,10 etc).

Some Macintosh users may run PC marine software on their Mac operating system using a PC or Windows 'emulator' program. These operate by providing a 'layer' between the Macintosh operating system, and the marine software. The marine software (written for Microsoft Windows) works with the emulator software, which translates the instructions to work with the Macintosh operating system 'underneath'. The Macintosh operating system in turn communicates directly with the Macintosh itself.

There are *caveats* with emulators, though: firstly, the emulator uses machine resources when running – your Mac may not have enough memory left to run its own operating system, the emulator program, Windows and the PC software at the same time. Also it quite simply may not work at an acceptable speed. Secondly, some PC programs require a dongle to be plugged into the PC's printer ('parallel') port, and Macs do not normally have this type of port fitted. Lastly, many marine programs use the PC's serial port to read data from the GPS; and whilst Macs have serial ports, connectors may differ or there may be compatibility problems.

There is no easy way to tell if an emulator will allow you to use a particular PC marine program on your Mac. The author's advice is to actually see the program (or at least a demonstration version) running on a Mac/emulator combination before parting with your money – since PC software is not intended to work on Macs, there may be a re-stocking fee if you return a system for this reason.

Unix and Linux

Another kind of normal PC is often termed simply a 'workstation'. These are very powerful machines (again, internally very different from the IBM compatible PC) typically to be found in scientific and research establishments.

These machines often run one of many different versions of an operating system family called Unix.

Regular Unix won't run on an IBM compatible PC, but a version that will, called Linux, has become commonplace, even popular.

Once again, software written for Microsoft Windows won't run on Linux unless an emulator is used. In this case, maybe because the underlying hardware is IBM compatible, programs seem to run quite well using Linux with a Windows emulator.

However, in keeping with Linux's scientific background, it can be quite complex to install and set up this operating system to work with various peripherals. The comments from the previous section regarding using emulators on Macintoshes apply with Unix or Linux as well, so the authors' advice, at least currently is to stick with the mainstream IBM/Windows combination.

Interestingly, as this book goes to press, a hybrid version of Linux and Windows – LindowsOS, has been announced, which promises to be able to run software written for both operating systems.

Appendix 2 ▪ Sources

The authors make no apologies for the fact that the following is not an exhaustive list of all possible suppliers.

The companies we have chosen for inclusion have been selected because, either as manufacturers or dealers, they have been active in this field for some time and are therefore probably the best equipped to give you good advice and service.

Manufacturer or dealer?

It may be thought that it is best to go direct to the manufacturers for some items, maybe in the hope of obtaining better pricing. This is often not the case: remember that they specialise in manufacturing, not end-user support, and that you may have to pay for technical support from the manufacturer whereas a dealer may include this as part of their service – always ask!

Specialist marine hardware and software dealers get good pricing from the manufacturers which enables them to be very competitive on price. When you also consider that they are experienced in installing, integrating and configuring a whole range of marine PC systems, they are much better placed than some manufacturers to provide a complete service and to offer good, unbiased advice.

As a final word, if you are planning to purchase anything to do with PCs, it is wise to contact as many suppliers as possible, and not just to confine yourself to the companies listed.

Computer manufacturers

Because of the large amount of computer brands currently available, it is impracticable to list them all here. Instead, the reader who is looking to buy a laptop or a desktop PC directly by mail order is advised to consult one of the many mainstream PC magazines. If you do not feel sufficiently knowledgeable to make this decision yourself, it is well worth contacting an experienced marine computing specialist who, for a small price premium, will be able to supply a PC that is suitable for your needs.

Such a specialist will also be aware of more rugged marinised units designed for use on board and which may not be widely advertised. The cost of these units is falling all the time and the market is changing rapidly, so ask lots of questions to make sure you are getting good advice.

Finally, though, as well as contacting the companies listed below, don't forget to try your usual chandlery – a few now have dedicated PCs and trained staff to demonstrate software products; and you, the customer, can encourage them by asking for these products.

All sources shown have been checked and were correct at time of going to press.

Aerohydro
PO Box 684   Tel: +1 (207) 244-4100
Southwest Harbour   Fax: +1 (207) 244-4171
ME 04679-0684   www.aerohydro.com
USA   info@aerohydro.com

* Computer Aided Design software

Andren Software
906 S Ramona Ave   Tel: +1 321 725 4115
Indialantic
FL 32903-3435   www.andren.com
USA   sales@andren.com

* LoranGPS – Loran-GPS conversion software

ARCS – See United Kingdom Hydrographic Office

Autoship Systems Corporation
Suit e 312   Tel: +1 (604) 254-4171
611 Alexander Street   Fax: +1 (602) 254-5171
Vancouver, BC   www.autoship.com
Canada V6A 1E1   sales@autoship.com

* marine software

Bonito
Gerichtsweg 3   Tel: +49 5052 6052
D-29320 Hermansburg   Fax: +49 5052 3477
Germany   www.bonito.net
                                    info@bonito.net

* Board Terminal – weatherfax/radio software
* Pro Meteo – weatherfax software

BSB – See Maptech UK Ltd

C-Map UK Ltd
Systems House   Tel: 01329 517777
Delta Business Park   Fax: 01329 517778
Salterns Lane   www.c-map.co.uk
Fareham   PO16 0QS UK   sales@c-map.co.uk

* C-Map electronic cartography (vector)

Celestaire
416 S Pershing
Wichita
KS 67218
USA

Tel: +1 (316) 686-9785
Fax: +1 (316) 686-8926
www.celestaire.com
info@celestaire.com

* Astro Navigation software

Creative Systems Inc
PO Box 1910
Port Townsend
WA 98368
USA

Tel: +1 (360) 385-6212
Fax: +1 (360) 385-6213
www.ghsport.com
sales@ghsport.com

* GHS – Trim and stability software

Dartcom
Powdermills
Postbridge
Yelverton
Devon PL20 6SP UK

Tel: 01822 880253
Fax: 01822 880232
www.dartcom.co.uk
dave@dartcom.co.uk

* Winsat Pro 32 Marine – weather satellite system and software

Dolphin Maritime Software Ltd
713 Cameron House
White Cross
South Road
Lancaster LA1 4XQ UK

Tel: 01524 841946
Fax: 01524 841946

* Marine software products for hand-held computers and PCs

Euronav Ltd
20 The Slipway
Port Solent
Portsmouth
PO6 4TR UK

Tel: 023 9237 3855
Fax: 023 9232 5800
www.euronav.co.uk
sales@euronav.co.uk

* seaPro 2000 – chart plotting system

Garmin (Europe) Ltd
Unit 5, The Quadrangle
Abbey Park Industrial Estate
Romsey
Hampshire SO51 9AQ UK

Tel: 01794 519944
Fax: 01794 519222
www.garmin.com

* GPS equipment

Global Navigation Software Co
5026 West Point Loma Blvd
San Diego
California 92107
USA

Tel: +1 619 225 0792

* NavPak chart plotting system

Globe Wireless
550 Pilgrim Avenue
Foster City
CA 94404
USA

Tel: +1 (650) 372-2650
Fax: +1 (650) 372-2656
www.globewireless.com
sales@globewireless.com

* Email over radio

Icom (UK) Ltd
Sea Street
Herne Bay
Kent CT6 8LD UK

Tel: 01227 741741
Fax: 01227 741742
www.icomuk.co.uk

* Conventional and PC controlled radio receivers and transceivers

ICS Electronics Ltd
Unit V
Rudford Industrial Estate
Ford
Arundel
West Sussex BN18 0BD UK

Tel: 01903 731101
Fax: 01903 731105
www.icselectronics.co.uk
sales@icselectronics.co.uk

* Fax 6 – weatherfax software
* WS5 – weather satellite system

Information Management Consultants
Media House
Mann Island
Liverpool L3 1DQ UK

Tel: 0151 236 4124
Fax: 0151 236 9907
www.super-hub.com

* Super-hub wireless data communications

Informatique et Mer
Technopole Izarbal
F-64210 Bidart
France

Tel: +33 559 43 81 00
Fax: +33 559 43 81 01
www.maxsea.com

* Maxsea – chart plotting software
* Macsea – chart plotting software for Macintosh
* Mapmedia – electronic charts (raster)

Kelvin Hughes
Kilgraston House
Southampton Street
Southampton
SO15 2ED UK

Tel: 023 8063 4911
Fax: 023 8033 0014
www.kh-online.co.uk

* Electronic charts and chart plotting software

Klas Ltd
Bracetown Business Park
Clonee
Co. Meath
Republic of Ireland

Tel: +353 1 6624270
Fax: +353 1 6624272
www.klasisdn.com

* PC interface cards for satellite communications

Lightmaster Software
18 Stanley Gardens
South Croydon
Surrey CR2 9AH UK

Tel: 020 8405 8200
Fax: 020 8405 8300
www.lightmaster.co.uk
sales@lightmaster.co.uk

* Interactive training and simulation software:
  covering lights, sounds, tides, VHF DSC, small craft radar

Livechart – see Euronav Ltd

Magellan – see Navicom SARL

Mapmedia – See Informatique et Mer

Maptech Inc
1 Riverside Drive
Andover
MA 01810-1122
USA

Tel: +1 888 839 5551
Fax: +1 978 933 3040
www.maptech.com

Maptech UK Ltd
The Book Barn
White Chimney Row
Westbourne
PO10 8RS UK

Tel: 01243 389352
Fax: 01243 379136
www.maptech.co.uk
sales@maptech.co.uk

* Offshore Navigator charting software
* Maptech BSB format electronic charts (raster)

Marine Computing International Ltd
Hamble Court
Hamble Lane
Southampton
SO31 4QJ UK

Tel: 023 8045 8047
Fax: 023 8045 8057
www.marinecomputing.com
sales@marinecomputing.com

* Complete range of marine software products
* Marine PCs and displays
* Interfacing and communications equipment
* Installation, configuration and training

Maritek
1-D7 Templeton Centre
Glasgow
G40 1DA UK

Tel: 0141 554 2492
Fax: 0141 639 1910
www.maritek.co.uk

* Tidal software for Psion hand-held computers
* Bosun – vessel management for Psion

Mastervolt UK Ltd
Winchester Hill Business Park
Romsey
Hants
SO51 7UT UK

Tel: 01794 516443
Fax: 01794 516453
www.mastervolt.co.uk
info@mastervolt.co.uk

* Inverters and battery chargers

Meridian Chartware Ltd
50 Unthank Road
Norwich
NR2 2RF UK

Tel: 01603 441026
Fax: 01603 765253
www.rcds.co.uk / dick@rcds.co.uk

* SEAtrak RCDS – chart plotting software

Merlin Equipment
Unit 1 Hithercroft Court
Lupton Road
Wallingford
OX10 9BT UK

Tel: 01491 824333
Fax: 01491 824466

* Inverters, AC and DC electrical generation and storage

Nautical Software – See Nobeltec

Nautical Technologies Ltd
217 Burleigh Road
Bangor
Maine 04401
USA

Tel: +1 207 942 4751
Fax: +1 207 941 1672
www.thecapn.com

* EasyNav – chart plotting software
* The Cap'n – chart plotting software

Navionics UK
PO Box 38
Plymouth
PL9 8YY UK

Tel: 01752 482632
Fax: 01752 481047
www.navionics.com

* Navionics electronic cartography (vector)

Neptune Navigation Software
PO Box 5106
Riseley
RG7 1FD UK

Tel: 0118 988 5309
Fax: 0870 0567329
www.neptune-navigation.com
sales@neptune-navigation.com

* Neptune – tides and tidal stream software
* Neptune – chart plotting and passage planning software

Navicom SARL
ZA des Boutries
Rue des Cayennes
78700 Conflans
France

Tel: +33 139 72 19 90
Fax: +33 139 19 28 98
www.navicom.fr
navicom@navicom.fr

* Magellan GPS distributors
* Mini-M Satellite phones

Nobeltec
15160 NW Laidlaw Road, Suite 100
Portland   Tel: +1 (503) 579-1414
OR 97229   Fax: +1 (503) 579-1304
USA   www.nobeltec.com
                                    sales@nobeltec.com

* Admiral – chart plotting software
* Visual Navigation Suite / Visual Mariner – chart plotting software
* Passport World Charts – vectorised charts
* Radar Solutions (with Koden & Anritsu transceivers)

Northport Systems Inc.
73 Warren Road   Tel: +1 416 920 0447
Toronto   Fax: +1 416 964 6313
Ontario   www.fugawi.com
Canada M4V 2R9

* Fugawi – chart plotting system

PC Maritime Ltd
Bain Clarkson House   Tel: 01752 254205
Brunswick Road   Fax: 01752 253599
Plymouth   www.pcmaritime.co.uk
PL4 0NP UK   aedmonds@pcmaritime.co.uk

* Navmaster – chart plotting software

PinOak Digital
PO Box 360   Tel: +1 908 234 2020
Gladstone   Fax: +1 908 234 9685
NJ 07934-0360   www.pinoak.com
USA

* HF radio communication and e-mail

Pinpoint Systems International
381-4 Old Riverhead Road   Tel: +1 516 288 0264
Westhampton Beach   Fax: +1 516 288 0294
New York 11978   www.pinpointsys.com
USA

* Softchart & NOS/GEO electronic cartography (raster)

Quintessence Designs
PO Box 228   Tel: +1 215 698 2424
Emporium   Fax: +1 978 383 6464
Pennsylvania 15834   www.quintessencedesigns.com
USA

* Range of marine software for the Macintosh

Raymarine
Anchorage Park
Portsmouth
PO3 5TD UK

Tel: 02392 693611
Fax: 02392 694642
www.raymarine.com

* Raytech – chart plotting software

SCS Mare Srl
Via Gandhi 29
20017 Mazzo di Rho
Milano
Italy

Tel: +39 02 939 09430
Fax: +39 02 939 09431
www.scsmare.com
info@scsmare.com

* Logbook – chart plotting software
* Alarm, monitoring, video surveillance software

Servowatch Systems
The Woodrope Building
Tollsebury
Essex
CM3 2EH UK

Tel: 01621 863583
Fax: 01621 862584
www.servowatch.co.uk
sales@servowatch.com

* Instrumentation logging and control systems for larger yachts

Transas Nautic
Sea Hawk
Bilton Way
Portsmouth
PO3 5JN UK

Tel: 023 9267 4016
Fax: 023 9267 4046
www.transasnautic.com
dataco@transas.co.uk

* Tsunamis NaviGator – chart plotting systems
* Transas TX97 – electronic charts (vector)

Trimble Navigation Europe Ltd
Meridian Office Park
Osborn Way
Hook RG27 9HX UK

Tel: 01256 760150
Fax: 01256 760148
www.trimble.com/sales/uk.htm

* GPS equipment

United Kingdom Hydrographic Office
1 Admiralty Way
Taunton
TA1 2DN UK

Tel: 01823 337900
Fax: 01823 323753
www.hydro.gov.uk

* ARCS raster charts

Victron Energie
Wheatfield Way
Hinckley Fields
Hinckley LE10 1YG UK

Tel: 01455 618666
Fax: 01455 611446
www.imv.co.uk

* Inverters and battery chargers

Glossary

Algorithm – A set of well-defined rules or operations designed to solve a particular problem reliably and efficiently

AM – Amplitude modulation. Where the carrier signal's amplitude (size) changes according to the frequency of an applied signal

ANSI – American National Standards Institute

ARCS – Admiralty raster chart service. Range of electronic raster versions of UKHO paper charts

ARPA – Automated radar plotting aid

ASCII – American Standard Code for Information Interchange. System whereby numbers, letters and symbols are expressed as numbers for easy processing by computers

Bandwidth – The amount of data that can be sent through a given communications system in a given period of time

Baud – Unit of signal frequency in signals per second. Not synonymous with bits per second because signals can represent more than one bit. Baud equals bits per second only when the signal represents a single bit

Binary – Characteristic of having only two states, such as on or off. The binary number system uses only ones and zeros

Bit – Binary digit. The basic unit of all digital communications. A bit is a 'one' or 'zero' in a binary language

BPS – Bits per second. A measure of transmission speed

Bus – Data interfacing system that joins PC components together

Byte – A data unit of eight bits

Carrier Signal – A continuous waveform (usually electrical) with properties capable of being modulated or impressed with a second information-carrying signal

CCITT – Committee Consultatif Internationale de Telegraphique et Telephonique. The International Telegraph and Telephone Consultative Committee, once part of the ITU

CD-ROM – Compact disc – read only memory

CRC – Cyclic redundancy check

CRT – Cathode ray tube. Traditional 'tube' used for TV or computer monitor display

CW – Carrier wave

DC – Direct current

DGPS – Differential GPS. A technique to improve GPS accuracy that uses pseudo-range errors recorded at a known location to improve the measurements made by other GPS receivers within the same general geographic area, with corrections transmitted over radio

Digital – The method of representing information as numbers with discrete (non continuous) values, usually expressed as a sequence of binary digits (ones and zeros)

DMA – Direct memory access or Defense Mapping Agency (US)

DoD – Department of Defense (US)

DRAM – Dynamic random access memory

Duplex – Characteristic of data transmission. Either full or half-duplex. Full permits simultaneous two-way communication. Half means only one side can talk at once

DVD – Digital versatile disk. A much higher capacity development of the CD-ROM, used for computer data storage and as a replacement for the video cassette

ECDIS – Electronic chart display and information system. A special term that refers to large ship bridge navigation systems conforming to standards laid down by the IMO

ECS – Electronic charting system. General term used to describe any computerised system capable of displaying electronic charts

EMC – Electromagnetic compatibility. The ability of electrical and electronic devices to work together without interference problems

ENC – Electronic navigational chart – A special term referring to electronic charts that conform to specific international standards for use with commercial ECDIS bridge systems

EPIRBs – Electronic Position Indicating Radio Beacons

ETSI – European Telecommunications Standards Institute. A counterpart to ANSI, facilitating integration of telecommunications standards into all of Europe and co-ordinating telecommunications policies

FAQ – Frequently asked questions.

FEC – Forward error correction. An error correction method used in data transmission

FM – Frequency modulation

FSK – Frequency shift keying modulation method

FTP – File transfer protocol. Internet service for up and downloading files efficiently

GMDSS – Global Maritime Distress and Safety System. A global standard for signalling and dealing with marine distress situations, using a combination of VHF, MF/HF radio, INMARSAT A, B and C

GMT – Greenwich Mean Time

GPS – Global positioning system. A series of satellites combined with specialised devices that allow you to pinpoint exact locations anywhere on the earth, typically, Longitude and Latitude. A space-based radio positioning system which provides suitably equipped users with accurate position, velocity and time data. GPS provides this data free of direct user charge worldwide, continuously and under all weather conditions. The GPS constellation consists of 24 orbiting satellites, four equally spaced around each of six different orbital planes

GSM – Global System for Mobile Communications, or Groupe Spéciale Mobile. A pan-European cellular phone system that allows European travellers to use a single cellular phone in many different countries and have all calls billed to one account. Adopted as the preferred cellular standard in Europe, Asia and North America

HCRF – Hydrographic Chart Raster Format. The standard created by the UKHO for their ARCS raster charts, now being adopted by other hydrographic offices as well

HDOP – Horizontal dilution of precision. A measure of how much the geometry of the GPS satellites affects the position estimate (computed from the satellite range measurements) in the horizontal East/North plane

Hz – Hertz. Unit of frequency

IEEE – Institute of Electrical and Electronics Engineers. A worldwide engineering publishing and standards-making body for the electronics industry

IHO – International Hydrographic Organisation

IMO – International Maritime Organisation. Intergovernmental organisation with responsibility for maintaining standards of safety at sea

INMARSAT – International Maritime Satellite Organisation

ISA – Industry Standard Architecture bus. The original PC bus, still fitted to machines but largely superseded by the PCI bus.

ISDN – Integrated Services Digital Network. A high speed data line (64kbps) used as an alternative to a normal phone line, and also available over the INMARSAT B system

ISO – International Standards Organisation. Devoted to determining standards for international and national data communications

ISP – Internet service provider. A company that gives the public access to the internet

ITU – International Telecommunications Union. An organisation established by the United Nations and having as its membership virtually every government in the world

ITU-T – International Telecommunications Union Telecommunications. An international body of member countries whose task is to define recommendations and standards relating to the international telecommunications industry. Has replaced the CCITT as the world's leading telecommunications standards organisation

kbps – Kilobits per second. A measure of transmission speed

kHz – Kilohertz. One thousand Hertz, or cycles, per second

LES – Land earth station. This station is the interface between a communications satellite and the land based phone system

Lithium Ion (Li-Ion) battery – An efficient battery technology, supporting relatively long standby and talk time with no memory effect

LOA – Length over all

LSB – Lower side band

Mbps – Megabits per second. A million bits per second, a measure of transmission speed

MHz – Megahertz. One million Hertz, or cycles per second

Modem – A device that links computers via telephone lines and enables the transmission of data. The name comes from 'modulate' and 'demodulate': a modem converts (modulates) the PC's signals from digital to analogue for transmission over telephone lines. At the other end, another modem converts them back (demodulates) from analogue to digital

Modulation – Superimposing data on top of a 'carrier' signal such that when the carrier signal is removed, the original data is left

Motherboard – Part of the computer system that includes data pathways between each major system component

MS-DOS – Microsoft Disk Operating System. A text-based operating system, common in the 1980s and early 1990s. In fact, Microsoft Windows 95 and 98 both run on top of a special version of MS-DOS, but it is mostly hidden from the user

MTBF – Mean time between failure. The average time a device runs until it fails

NiCad – Nickel cadmium. A type of battery

NiMH – Nickel metal hydride. A type of battery

NMEA – National Marine Electronics Association (US)

NMEA0183 – A standard protocol deviced by the NMEA to enable instruments to communicate with each other (and also with computers)

NOAA – US National Oceanographic and Aeronautical Administration

Non-volatile (memory) see NVRAM

NVRAM – Non-volatile random access memory

OEM – Original equipment manufacturer

Opto-isolator – A device used to help eliminate electrical interference, and also to protect devices from electrical surges down data cables. It is required to be fitted on the receive side of all NMEA0183 interfaces.

Packet – A bundle of data, usually in binary form, organised in a specific way for transmission. Three principal elements are included in the packet: 1, control information such as destination, origin and length of packet; 2, the data to be transmitted; and 3, error-detection and correction bits

Parallel port – A port used for interfacing to printers and other devices. A number of data lines are used to send multiple items of data at once, as opposed to a serial port where the data just goes down one data line

PC Card (formerly PCMCIA card). Credit sized cards for use with laptop PCs, defined by the PCMCIA standard. The PCMCIA standards include three types, distinguished by increasing thickness: type 1: very thin memory cards, seldom used, type 2: most modems and interfaces; type 3: double thickness cards used for disk drives.

PCB – Printed circuit board

PCI – The standard bus for internal PC expansion cards, much faster than the ISA bus also installed in most machines.

PCMCIA – See PC Card

Protocol – A specific set of rules, procedures or conventions relating to format and timing of data transmission between two devices

Psion – A manufacturer of hand held computers, with their own proprietary operating system

PSTN – Public switched telephone network. Usually refers to the worldwide voice telephone network accessible to all those with telephones and access privileges. The PSTN is a gigantic maze of switching computers that can connect any two telephone points in potentially hundreds of different ways

RAM – Random access memory. Read-write volatile memory that is lost when power is discontinued; temporary storage

Raster – An image represented as a regular grid of different colour pixels. In charts, used to refer to scanned in charts

RS232 – The standard protocol used for serial ports on PCs

RS422 – A serial data standard used by Macintosh computers and also an element of the NMEA specification

SA – Selective availability. The method used by the DoD to control access to the full GPS accuracy

SCSI – Small computer systems interface. An interface used for high performance hard disks, CD-ROM drives and some other peripherals

SMS – Short message service. Enables a GSM phone to send a short text message to another GSM phone

SOLAS – Safety of life at sea

SSB – Single side band

Synchronous – Signals that are sourced from the same timing reference and have the same frequency; events that happen at the same time with respect to network timing

TCP/IP – Transmission Control Protocol/Internet Protocol. The network protocol used for the internet and for many local area computer networks

TFT – Thin film transistor. Technology used to produce flat panel computer and TV displays

UHF – Ultra high frequency

UKHO – United Kingdom Hydrographic Office

USB – Universal serial bus. A method of linking numerous external devices to a PC

USB – Upper side band

UTC – Universal Time Coordinated. This time system uses the second defined true angular rotation of the earth measured as if the earth rotated about its conventional terrestrial pole. However, UTC is adjusted only in increments of 1 second. The time zone of UTC is that of GMT

Vector – A line defined by its start point, direction and length. In terms of charts, vector charts refer to charts where the data is held in a database of points, lines, areas and symbols.

VHF – Very high frequency

Volatile (memory) – memory whose contents are lost when the power is switched off, for example the memory chips installed in PCs

WGS84 – World Geodetic System (1984). A mathematical ellipsoid designed to fit the shape of the entire earth. It is often used as a reference on a worldwide basis, while other ellipsoids are used locally to provide a better fit to the earth in a local region. GPS uses the centre of the WGS84 ellipsoid as the centre of its reference frame

Index

S

satcom, 16
satellite, 55
satellite TV services, 64
satphone, 62
SCSI interface, 97
secondary ports, 49
security key, 26
Selective Availability (SA), 30
serial port, 106
sextant altitude, 54
shielded network cabling (STP), 133
ship earth station (SES), 60
shock, 116
SIMM memory, 100
Simplified Harmonic Method (SHM), 49
simulators, 82
sine-wave inverter, 120
SODIMM memory, 100, 136
Softchart, 25
software, 95
Splitting NMEA0183 signals, 131
SSB, 59, 67
SVGA, 103
SYNOP, 70
synoptic, 67
system software, 13
systems monitoring, 78

T

talker (NMEA) 45, 129
TCP/IP, 88
Teledesic, 65
Telex Over Radio (TOR), 59
Telnet, 89
temperature, 116
TFT displays, 86, 114, 118, 125
Thuraya, 63
Tidal heights, 38
Tidal passage planning, 50
Tide height prediction, 47
touch-screen, 105, 106
trackball, 105
training software, 81, 82
Transas, 25
Transmeta, 98
tri-band phone, 56
tutor software, 84
TV and video playback, 86, 125

U

UK Hydrographic Office (UKHO), 25
UK Meteorological Office (UKMO), 69
Ultra ATA/100, 97
Uninterruptible Power Supplies, 124
Unix, 110, 140
unlock codes, 26
unshielded network cabling (UTP), 133
updating services, 32
upgrading, 135
upload, 37
USB, 13, 27, 97, 98, 108

V

vector charts, 19
Velcro, 113
vertical datum, 29
vessel administration, 77
vessel following, 36
vibration, 116
video monitoring, 80
video splitter, 124
virtual pilotage, 52

W

warping, 31
waypoints, 28, 33, 34
weather routeing, 37
weather satellite, 72
Weatherfax, 67
webcams, 80
Wefax, 72
WGS84 datum, 29
WiFi, 134
Windows emulators, 139
wired networks, 133
wireless networks, 134
workstation, 140
World Meteorological Organisation, 70
World Wide Web (WWW), 87, 90

X

XGA, 103

Z

Zip drive, 102

Free Demonstration CD-ROM Voucher

The authors have prepared a companion CD-ROM to this book. The CD-ROM contains free software, trial versions and demonstrations of a range of marine software.

If you would like to receive a copy of this CD-ROM, absolutely free of charge in the UK, complete this form and post it in an envelope to:

Over The Horizon (dept UPCOB 2)
PO Box 5192
Bridport
DT6 4XZ
United Kingdom

If you have access to the Internet and prefer not to cut this voucher out of the book, simply complete the on-screen form at the following web address: http://www.over-the-horizon.co.uk/upcob2/democd.htm

Please allow 28 days for delivery

Initials: _____ Surname: _____

Address: _____

_____

Town: _____ Postcode: _____

Country: _____

Daytime Telephone: _____

E-mail address: _____

Please complete the following questions:

Boat owner?   Y/N   If so, size LOA: _____ ft/m

Manufacturer?   eg Oyster, Fairline, one-off _____

Sailing area? _____

Do you own a: Desktop PC? Y/N   Laptop PC? Y/N   Rugged PC? Y/N

Do you use a PC on your boat?   Y/N

Is it a ❏ laptop   or ❏ permanently fixed?

Age group?   13–21 ❏   22–34 ❏   35–44 ❏   45–54 ❏   55–64 ❏   65+ ❏